GILL'S IRISH LIVES

ARTHUR GRIFFITH

CALTON YOUNGER

GILL AND MACMILLAN

First published 1981 by
Gill and Macmillan Ltd
Goldenbridge
Dublin 8
with associated companies in
London, New York, Delhi, Hong Kong,
Johannesburg, Lagos, Melbourne,
Singapore, Tokyo.

0 7171 1011 7 (paperback)
0 7171 1073 7 (hardback)

available in this series:
Michael Collins (Leon Ó Broin)
Sean O'Casey (Hugh Hunt)
C. S. Parnell (Paul Bew)
James Craig (Patrick Buckland)
James Joyce (Peter Costello)
Eamon de Valera (T. Ryle Dwyer)
Daniel O'Connell (Fergus O'Ferrall)
Theobald Wolfe Tone (Henry Boylan)
Edward Carson (A. T. Q. Stewart)
James Connolly (Ruth Dudley Edwards)
Arthur Griffith (Calton Younger)

Origination by Healyset, Dublin
Printed and bound in Great Britain by
Redwood Burn Ltd., Trowbridge, Wiltshire.

Contents

1
The Matrix

Arthur Griffith believed that Ireland's freedom could be won by peaceful means, and he may have been right. It is more likely that if there had been no Easter Rising he would be remembered today as an inspired journalist and skilful publicist, and that Sinn Féin would have been no more than an eccentric footnote in history.

The Ireland into which he was born, on 31 March 1871, was not so much peaceful as stunned. Only a generation earlier, famine had struck her down; Ireland's population had been reduced by over two million as people either fled from hunger or died of it. Not that there was a shortage of food. Only the potato crop had failed, but because of the deep-rooted injustice of the system of land tenure, and a combination of callousness and muddled economic thinking, the bulk of Ireland's varied agricultural produce was exported to England.

Just over seventy years before Griffith was born, an event occurred which was to set the pattern of his life. By dubious but by no means secret means, William Pitt and Lord Castlereagh, Prime Minister and Irish Chief Secretary, respectively, had procured the Act of Union (1800) and Ireland lost her own parliament, the independence of which, achieved as recently as 1782, had been recognised by an Act of Renunciation of the British parliament the following year. The parliament of Ireland was by no means a model institution.

It could still be manipulated from England through
[2] the corrupt system of 'rotten boroughs', and it represented only the Protestant ruling class.

Henry Grattan, born in 1746, was the outstanding Irish political leader of the time and directed the Irish parliament's movement to win independence. He was a strong advocate of Catholic emancipation. 'The Irish Protestant can never be free whilst the Catholic is a slave,'[1] he said. He sought to remove other abuses, but universal suffrage was far from his mind. On the contrary, he wanted 'to combat the wild spirit of democratic liberty by the regulated spirit of organised liberty'.[2] He had no desire to sever ties with Britain; he saw the two countries as independent but connected, through historical association, by allegiance to the same monarch.

The destruction of Ireland's parliament changed the course of history. For Arthur Griffith, though he fastened upon the later parallel of Hungary to make his point, Grattan's parliament was the key to the political philosophy he developed and formulated, from which he was convinced Irish independence could evolve and which finally provided the scaffolding for the building of a revolution.

Arthur Griffith was the son and grandson of printers. His grandfather came of a Protestant farming family in the Ulster county of Monaghan, but having espoused the Catholic faith at an early age he was no longer welcome at home and sought his fortune in Dublin. He married relatively young, apparently was reasonably successful in his trade and moved to Naas in Co. Kildare. His son, Arthur, married a girl named Mary Whelan, set up house in Dominick Street in the heart of Dublin and named his own son after himself. As the family increased in number and the family finances became stretched, the Griffiths moved to Little Britain Street and the young Arthur, nicknamed 'Dan', received what formal education he had at a Christian Brothers' school. [3]

To a gifted youngster like Arthur Griffith, the education he searched out for himself was of far greater importance than schoolroom tuition. No doubt he made the most of his opportunities at school and certainly he came under the influence of Brother Morrissey, a redoubtable teacher with a deep belief in Irish nationalism and a vast comprehension of Irish history.

The bones of Griffith's remarkable intellect came from profound reading and were fleshed out by almost interminable debate and discussion. He had a way with words, not the magic of O'Casey or Shaw, perhaps, but a gift for the unexpected cadence, the penetrating phrase. His cavernous memory accommodated comfortably not only all that he gleaned from his greedy reading, including a detailed knowledge of Irish place names and topography, but tunes picked up from the buskers and balladists on the streets of Dublin. His mother's was a musical family and Griffith delighted in music throughout his life.

Leaving school at fifteen, Arthur Griffith was apprenticed to a small family firm of printers run by Miss Jane Underwood, a middle-aged lady with a caring nature and a love of books. She soon perceived the quality of the young apprentice and, while he learned his trade as a compositor, she interested him in reading, lending him books and discussing them with him.

Sometimes he drew on his well-stocked memory to show off a little when, with fellow apprentices, he promenaded the evening streets and flirted with idling groups of girls. Scorning the usual routine of banter, he would launch into a long quotation from Shakespeare, bemusing his chosen companion of the moment. Padraic Colum, to whom Bob Mangan, one of Griffith's fellow apprentices, told the story, remarks: 'Very likely the youngster's display of erudition was as much to

cover his shyness as to make an impression.'[3] That
[4] shyness was innate and thickened into a reserve which many found forbidding.

In the Ireland of his youth his questing mind was matched by many. The youngsters of the Fireside Clubs, inspired by the poet Rose Kavanagh, met by candlelight in rented rooms, for which often they could not pay, to talk about books and about Ireland. They learned from writers like Thomas Davis (1814–45) and John Mitchel (1815–75). Griffith attracted a coterie of apprentices, who debated in doorways far into the night. By the time he was seventeen he was running the Eblana Literary and Debating Society, which soon merged with the Leinster Literary Society. Under the name of 'Shanganagh', one of many pseudonyms he was to use in his working life, he contributed to a fortnightly journal, *Eblana*, which first appeared on 8 February 1889 and ran for seven issues, all handwritten. Explaining that the society was 'composed of hard working young men of humble circumstances who formed a society for their mutual improvement', the editor enjoined any stranger reading the paper to remember that it was written 'by youths to fortune and to fame unknown'.[4]

Arthur Griffith had been impelled to write from an early age and his contributions to *Eblana* were well constructed, though negligibly punctuated, and revealed an incipient political awareness. In an essay on 'Irish Street Ballads' he wrote:

> The street ballad vigorously assailed 'The Union' project. Pleasant Ned Lysaght wrote many fine ballads against that villainous scheme which enjoyed great popularity one of them was prophetic of Dublin if the Union was carried.
>
> 'Down Grafton Street now as ye secretly range
> You'll scarce recognise it as the same street

White turnips will grow in the Royal Exchange
And cabbages down along Dame Street.' [5]

But alas despite Lysaght's songs the bill was carried.

In another, somewhat facetious, essay, 'The Vagaries of a Printer', Griffith obviously drew on his own experiences, backed up by research. Beginning with 'The compositor being little more than an ordinary mortal shares in common with his fellow men the liability of making a mistake now and then . . .' he then gave examples of amusing misprints for which he had searched through publications dating back to 1854. In the same issue of *Eblana* Griffith wrote knowledgably of guerrilla warfare in Wicklow and Wexford in 1978 and of the leaders, Holt, Michael Dwyer and William Byrne.

It was at a meeting of the Leinster Literary Society that Griffith met William Rooney who, at sixteen, was a veteran of the Fireside Clubs. They had been at the same school but, senior by a year, Griffith did not remember the younger lad. Almost at once, it seemed, he saw in Rooney a leader to whom he was ready to give his allegiance. The two became fast friends. But if Rooney was a star on the horizon, the immediate blazing sun was Charles Stewart Parnell.

Parnell had entered parliament in 1875. Born in 1846, the year famine struck Ireland, he was a handsome scion of an aristocratic Protestant family. Although early in his career, perhaps at Cambridge, he conceived an intense dislike of England and the English, in temperament and character he seemed essentially of the English upper crust himself. Parnell became chairman of the Home Rule party in May 1880. Although never very forthcoming about his political aims and no innovator, his leadership brought a new dynamism to the political fray.

Making his first priority reform of the pernicious land system as a necessary prelude to self-government,

Parnell became chairman of the National Land League
[6] of Ireland, founded by Michael Davitt in 1879 when famine once again threatened disaster. Gladstone's Land Act of 1881 and measures passed by Salisbury's Conservative administration in 1887 and 1891 eased but did not wholly solve the problem.

Home Rule was the main issue in Ireland in the general election of 1885 when the Irish Parliamentary Party won 85 of 103 seats. Under Parnell it had become streamlined and efficient – 'the first British democratic political machine of modern times'.[5]

Parnell flirted with the Conservatives but Lord Salisbury's idea of Home Rule came nowhere near Parnell's and it was left to Gladstone to introduce his bill in 1886. It was too much for some Liberals and Gladstone, defeated, resigned. But it was an achievement of both Gladstone and Parnell that a bill to give Ireland Home Rule was brought to the House at all. Furthermore, the lines had been drawn. Home Rule was a clear issue between the two main political parties in England.

In 1890, Parnell's ten-year liaison with Kitty O'Shea, wife of one of his MPs, came to light when the husband, complaisant until then, started divorce proceedings. At first it seemed that little had been lost. The Irish Parliamentary Party voted Parnell their support at a meeting in Dublin which the young Arthur Griffith attended. Then, under pressure from various quarters in England, Gladstone warned Parnell publicly that, if he remained as leader, the Liberals would lose the next election and with it any hope of Home Rule legislation. Parnell did not resign but his party came to pieces in his hands and was to remain hopelessly divided for nine years.

Arthur Griffith, nineteen years old when Parnell's star fell, stayed faithful to his hero. Anxious to prove that he had the confidence of the Irish people, Parnell put three supporters forward in by-elections, but none was successful. Griffith thought that Parnell himself [7] should contest a seat in Dublin.

Timothy Harrington MP was surprised when Griffith called at his home and asked him to resign his seat to allow Parnell to stand for election. 'What Dublin says today, all Ireland will say tomorrow,' the young man told him. Harrington declined politely but was curious about his visitor. As it happened, a messenger called as Griffith was leaving and was able to tell Harrington that he had heard Griffith speaking in favour of Parnell at a meeting of students and workers at Stephen's Green a few evenings earlier.[6] Parnell married his Kitty O'Shea but died a year later at the age of forty-five.

In 1892, Gladstone formed another government, his precarious majority dependent on the support of the Irish Nationalists. Bravely he steered his second Home Rule Bill through the House of Commons the following year, but he could have seen it only as breaking a little more ground, for there was no possibility of support for the measure in the House of Lords.

The young men of the Leinster Literary Society remained staunchly in the Parnellite camp, but the 'uncrowned king' of Ireland was dead and nowhere in sight was there a leader of anything like the same stature. William Rooney, perhaps? It was at this point that, precociously, Arthur Griffith began, as he wrote later, 'to build my hopes for Ireland on him and to regard him as the destined regenerator of his people'.[7] Griffith's first published works were in collaboration with Rooney, a series of articles in the *Evening Herald* entitled 'Notable Graves in and around Dublin'. The sepulchral theme was simply a device to allow them to write about great Irishmen of the past.

Earnest discussion and debate and readings of papers and poems, mostly in the mould of the Young Irelanders, were not the only activities of the Leinster

Literary Society. There were musical evenings, too,
[8] and on one occasion two sisters, Maud and Annie Sheehan, helped with the entertainment. Both were talented, Annie especially, but it was the fifteen-year old Maud who took Griffith's eye and eventually won his heart. The Sheehans were a well-to-do family and the diffident Griffith, who became a frequent caller, must have been rather overawed. He was never able to offer her the lifestyle she knew and it was to be many years before he could offer even a modicum of security. Colum reproduces a letter Griffith wrote to Maud Sheehan on 18 January 1894.

> Dear Miss Sheehan,
>
> The 'Lily of Killarney' is announced for Saturday night. Do you remember your promise? If you are not better engaged for that evening, I would be delighted to meet you at, say, a quarter past seven o'clock at the corner of Winetavern Street and Merchant's Quay.
>
> Sincerely yours,
> Arthur Griffith.

Colum comments: 'The shyness that was so noticeable in Griffith is in this note.' There is more, too, the innate courtesy and the facility with words. One only wonders why he did not offer to call for her.

The Leinster Literary Society was almost bored to death by a member, older than most, who insisted on reciting great chunks of Thomas Moore. Rooney led the rest of the members into a new society, the Celtic Literary Society, leaving the proser in sole possession of the outworn Leinster. The new society, with Rooney as president, took up quarters in Lower Abbey Street.

It was here that Griffith first met William Butler Yeats, brought by Maud Gonne with whom Yeats had fallen in love in 1889 and whose extreme nationalist views had fired his own enthusiasm for the cause.

Maud Gonne described Arthur Griffith as 'a fair, shy boy one would hardly notice'.[8] Yet she was attracted [9] to him and he soon became a member of her circle. At the time he was a copyreader on the *Irish Independent* and the physical characteristics by which people were to remember him had set. Of something less than medium height, he was of chunky build – 'square' was a word frequently used to describe him. Beneath a broad forehead his face had a pugnacious set, the jaw firm, the nose large but well-shaped. Thick glasses detracted from penetrating blue eyes in which there was a glint of ironical humour, hinted at in the mouth also and emphasised in his later years by the slight twirl of heavy moustache.

Intellectually he still had a long way to go but, as a member of Maud Gonne's group, he found himself mixing with people who honed the blade of his mind. Apart from Maud Gonne and Yeats, there was Douglas Hyde, one of the founders of the Gaelic League, an Irish scholar and poet from Co. Roscommon, eight years Griffith's senior; James Connolly, whose dream it was to transform Ireland into a socialist republic; and John O'Leary, a venerable Fenian, born in 1830, and once a Young Irelander. For him, as for Griffith, Thomas Davis was a constant inspiration and, as Davis's near contemporary, O'Leary had much to offer the younger man.

Arthur Griffith must have found the milieu in which he moved exciting and he was beginning to make a reputation for himself. He was someone to watch. Yet now he chose to leave it all behind.

2
Home Thoughts from Abroad

Towards the end of 1897, when he was twenty-six, Griffith sailed in the *Norman Castle* for South Africa. He went partly for health reasons, there being some suspicion that he had inherited a family proclivity to tuberculosis, partly because the printing trade had become somewhat precarious, and partly no doubt because he wished to open his mind to new vistas.

Disembarking at Lourenço Marques, he made his way by train to Pretoria where, as a journeyman compositor, he found employment in his own trade. Apparently his reputation as a writer and publicist had preceded him, for he was soon invited to take over the running of a weekly paper in Middleburg in the heart of the Transvaal. It was called *Courant* and, until Griffith's advent as editor, the policy of the paper was, more or less, to offend no-one.

'I explained to the owner,' wrote Griffith, 'that if he wanted me to edit the paper its policy must be one which would please myself by arguing that the Boer and no one but the Boer owned the Transvaal, and that the Queen's writ didn't run there, and that God Almighty had not made the earth for the sole use of the Anglo-Saxon race.'[1]

Relations between the British and the Boers had been irrevocably soured long before Griffith's arrival in the Transvaal and a strongly pro-Boer English newspaper was hardly likely to attract readers. *Courant* was soon no more. Back in Pretoria, Griffith felt totally at ease among the Boer community and came to hero-worship Paul Kruger, whose neighbour for a time he was. Interesting himself in the political and economic framework of the country, he was charmed by the amiability of the presidential election of 1898 when Kruger defeated two rivals – Schalk-Burgher and Joubert. He used to watch them in the evening 'drinking their coffee, smoking their pipes and chatting and laughing together on the President's stoep ...'[2]

However, Griffith never lost sight of the real aim of his life, the liberation of Ireland from the British, and he was eager to learn as much as he could from the pious and sturdy Dutchmen in whose midst he moved. He was in constant touch with William Rooney, who kept him informed about Dublin's preparations to celebrate the centenary anniversary of the 1798 rebellion, and he quickly made friends with members of Pretoria's Irish community.

It was in Johannesburg, to which Griffith moved for the sake of more lucrative employment, that he met John MacBride. The two, with another Irishman named Whelan, a member of the Celtic Literary Society, were instrumental in creating an Irish Society, Griffith making it plain to his countrymen that they should not be linked, in the minds of the Boer community, with the people whom they both despised and whose flag was an affront to their heritage.

Griffith was determined that the centenary of '98 should be celebrated in Johannesburg and a splendid parade was organised. It took place on the same day as the Dublin celebration and people of many nationalities joined the lustily singing Irish contingent. Almost every European country was pro-Boer as antagonism between the Boers and the British festered, and their nationals in the Transvaal, mostly drawn there by the lure of gold, were anxious to show whose side they were on.

A month after his Johannesburg triumph, Griffith
[12] returned to Ireland. The Irish Society, many of whose members were Irish-Americans, became a military unit on the outbreak of the Boer War in October 1899 and led, first by a former United States officer and then by John MacBride, fought with the Boers. Sustained by every farmhouse, familiar with every contour of the countryside, the Boers fought the war against the British in small, highly mobile groups specialising in surprise attacks. Avoiding the formal battlefield scenario, they were singularly successful, and less then twenty years later the Irish were to adapt their methods to their own terrain.

In Dublin Arthur Griffith took a leading role in forming 'The Transvaal Committee' whose purpose was to enlist public sympathy for the Boers and to discourage young Irishmen from joining the British army. It was planned also to send a manned ambulance to help the Boers. Maud Gonne, who had presided over the formation of the Transvaal Committee, mounted a perfervid anti-recruiting campaign.

Another stalwart of the Transvaal Committee was James Connolly, a fervent socialist who had come to Ireland in 1896 from Scotland. Connolly saw the Boer War as a chance to undermine Britain's power in Ireland and he prepared a plan to capture certain buildings in Dublin, a plan which strikingly resembles that of the Easter Rising of 1916. Connolly argued that there were only 25,000 troops in Ireland and that this was the time to strike. Very reasonably, Griffith pointed to the lack of Irish arms. 'Have your revolution first and the arms will come afterwards,' said Connolly.[3] The model for revolution in Connolly's mind was that of certain European countries. Griffith remained unconvinced. He pointed out that, in those countries, what Connolly called a revolution was in reality a domestic uprising with a proportion of the army siding with the revolutionaries. In Ireland the situation was very different; the people were totally unprepared and unaccustomed to the use of arms; the country was occupied by foreign soldiers. Griffith added that the British navy could bombard Irish towns. Connolly was sceptical. A capitalist government would never destroy capitalist property, he maintained, but Griffith was sure that Irish property, capitalist or not, did not count. Disgruntled, Connolly had little to do with the nationalists from then on, though Griffith and he remained on good terms.

The Transvaal Committee reacted swiftly to the announcement that Joseph Chamberlain, Secretary of State for the Colonies, was to visit Dublin. Once regarded as a dangerous Radical, Chamberlain had vigorously opposed Gladstone's Home Rule Bills of 1886 and 1893. So effective was the protest orchestrated by the Transvaal Committee that Chamberlain's visit was watered down from official to semi-official and then to private. Even that was seen as an affront by Griffith and his friends, who organised a protest meeting for Sunday, 17 December. One of the speakers was to be the revered old Fenian, John O'Leary. On the Saturday night, a meeting, chaired by William Redmond, was held to make final arrangements. Officers of the Dublin Metropolitan Police (DMP) interruped the conclave and announced that the protest meeting planned for the morrow had been proclaimed. Copies of the proclamation were handed around and angrily Griffith tore his up and threw it on the fire.

Griffith urged defiance and the committee agreed to go ahead but, when he called on John O'Leary, he found, to his consternation, that O'Leary was against the meeting taking place. Was Griffith able to defend the people, he wanted to know. How did he propose to

fight the police and perhaps the army? Griffith was
[14] bewildered. He intended to fight no-one. 'We may be prevented from holding our meeting by England's armed forces. We shall prove that her power here rests on force,' he replied.[4]

If Griffith hoped to avoid violence, Connolly welcomed the thought of a scrap. 'The people must become case-hardened to conflict,' he pronounced. 'People don't become case-hardened to being dead,' Griffith retorted.[5]

Of the several speakers advertised only the unquenchable Maud Gonne was ready to go on. A brake had been hired, but when he saw her the driver scented trouble and refused to drive. Connolly grabbed the reins. A crowd had gathered near the Custom House and the police had formed a cordon. Lashing the horses to a gallop and with the crowd cheering, Connolly rammed a way through the cordon. He began to address the crowd, some of whom impeded the police and were thwacked by irate batons. The brake was seized and its occupants escorted to Store Street police station. There they were told that if they wanted to hold a meeting they should have it outside the city boundary.

They set off again. Large crowds in Talbot Street formed a procession behind the brake. There was a profusion of Irish and Boer flags. The procession grew and the police gave up any attempt to keep order. Twelve brakes full of policemen arrived and joined the procession. Griffith was gleeful: 'We moved off again followed by the twelve brakes laden with the richly uniformed policemen, so that our demonstration was greatly improving in appearance'.[6]

Near Parliament Street, police wearing silver and blue uniforms and plumed helmets charged the crowd, using the flats of their swords. Incensed, the crowd counter-attacked with a variety of weapons begged from houses in the street. Griffith struggled with a police officer – who was trying to seize a Boer flag from a small boy. George Lyons saw the officer and his horse sprawling in the road, while Griffith triumphantly waved the flag in one hand, the officer's sword in the other.

In Capel Street, Connolly, Griffith and Maud Gonne were arrested but argued convincingly that they were driving to their rooms in Abbey Street, that they were not holding a meeting and that it was the police themselves who were causing all the excitement. The police allowed themselves to be persuaded, or perhaps they had a sneaking sympathy for the agitators, so the party went on its way and the crowd followed. At 32 Lower Abbey Street, the home of the Celtic Literary Society, the missing speakers, including O'Leary, joined the demonstrators – 'the careful clique' Connolly called them. He himself tried to continue the joy-ride but this time the police had had enough. He was charged with driving without a licence and subsequently was fined £2. Maud Gonne paid.

Arthur Griffith, too, had a brush with the law at this time and spent two weeks in Mountjoy rather than pay a fine for assaulting one Ramsay Colles, editor of *Irish Figaro,* a gossip magazine, to whom he had traced ludicrous rumours that Maud Gonne was in the pay of the Castle. Griffith was not given to violence and has often been regarded as a pacifist, but he did not shrink from violence when he believed it was justified.

Earlier in 1899, Arthur Griffith and William Rooney founded a weekly newspaper, the *United Irishman,* naming it after Mitchel's revolutionary paper of 1847. Written almost entirely by the impecunious but ambitious pair, the first issue appeared on 4 March 1899. Their intention was to light the path to independence,

to bring together in a homogeneous national movement
[16] the various political factions and patriotic groups who were reviving the Irish language and Irish culture which, through the greater part of the century, had been overlaid by English ways, in particular by the introduction of the English system of primary education.

It was a time when England's grip on the country had yielded a little. Gladstone's first action on coming to power in 1868 had been to disestablish the Anglican church in Ireland the following year. The several Land Acts had gone some way to rectify the injustices suffered by Irish tenants. The grand juries of the Ascendancy, which had controlled local government for more than two hundred years, were replaced in 1898 by elected county and district councils. This certainly was an improvement but fell short of Gladstone's ill-fated Home Rule measure of 1893. Various other reforms also were introduced in these years and the Irish smelt freedom on the wind. If there was a lesson to be learned from the fall of Parnell and the disintegration of the Parliamentary Party, it was that the Irish owed Britain nothing, least of all gratitude for ameliorating the conditions Britain herself had created.

The Gaelic League, formed in 1893 to revive the fading Irish language by three like-minded scholars, Douglas Hyde, Father Eugene O'Growny and Eoin Mac Néill, soon attracted a tremendous following; the Gaelic Athletic Association, founded by Michael Cusack in Thurles in 1884, resisted the anglicisation of recreation and promoted indigenous games and had, incidentally, a firm link with the Fenians. These, with the National Literary Society, founded in 1892 by W. B. Yeats and T. W. Rolleston, manifested a resurgence not just of nationalist spirit but of confidence in Irish civilisation and culture.

Hyde was anxious to keep the Gaelic League out of the political arena but Rooney and Griffith could not accept that any organisation whose aim was to preserve the national identity could eschew politics. They saw Irish literature in the context of nationalism, best exemplified by the work of Thomas Davis who, with John Blake Dillon and Charles Gavan Duffy, formed the nucleus of the 'Young Ireland' group and in 1842 launched their own newspaper, *The Nation*.

Yeats saw Davis as a stultifying influence and urged the freedom of the artist from the chains of patriotism. 'If creative minds preoccupy themselves with incidents from the political history of Ireland, so much the better, but we must not force them to select those incidents,' he wrote in the *United Irishman*.[7]

Yeats often contributed to the *United Irishman* and was a frequent caller at its editor's office. Griffith was not so hidebound that he could not appreciate the power and beauty of Yeats's poetry: 'Mr Yeats sings of what he knows and sings more beautifully than ever Irish poet sang before . . .' he wrote.[8]

Like Yeats, Griffith had joined the Irish Republican Brotherhood, yet another segment of the rambling nationalist movement. The IRB was to spearhead the physical force movement which in time was to coalesce with virtually every other group which had as its aim a free and independent Ireland, but at this time it was moribund. It had been formed in 1958, both in Ireland and America and was given the name of the Fenian Brotherhood in America by John O'Mahony. In 1873, following the ill-starred insurrection of '67, the society was reorganised and became the Irish Republican Brotherhood, though the word Fenian was still used to denote the physical force movement.

How much Griffith's thinking was influenced by his membership of the organisation is problematical, but the *United Irishman* had made a distinct impact and Griffith's ideas were becoming familiar through the many groups concerned with the political and cultural future of their country. It had attracted a variety of contributors and would-be contributors, particularly after the first waspish year in which caustic criticism rather than constructive suggestion had pervaded its pages, though the gentler Rooney had leavened them with idealistic essays which drew heavily on Thomas Davis.

Griffith was still much preoccupied with the events in South Africa where his friend John MacBride was leading an Irish Brigade. When, as a protest against the Boer War, Michael Davitt resigned his parliamentary seat in South Mayo, Griffith and Rooney thought to double the force of his protest by nominating MacBride as a candidate in the by-election. Sponsored by the Transvaal Committee, the absent MacBride was put forward as an independent nationalist and was soundly defeated by the Parliamentary Party candidate. Shortly afterwards, in April 1900, at the height of the Boer War, the aged Queen Victoria visited Dublin. Irish nationalists deplored her visit which they regarded simply as a recruiting gimmick. Griffith wrote contemptuously of the visit but vast numbers of people welcomed her, including John Redmond who was proud of the deeds of Irish soldiers fighting the Boers. A gigantic party was given for school children to celebrate her coming and Maud Gonne organised a rival 'National Treat' for the children of nationalist parents who wanted none of the Queen's beneficence. Griffith, in paper hat, happily played with Maud Gonne's protegés.

As the nineteenth century neared its end, the splinter groups of the Parliamentary Party began to come together again. John Redmond was elected chairman. Reunited, they were ready to pursue the elusive goal of Home Rule, but unless at some point the party held the balance of power in the House of Commons, there was little likelihood that self-government would be won by what the party regarded as constitutional, and Griffith as unconstitutional, means. But, at that time, the majority of the Irish people, even if they had heard of the obscure Griffith, counted him for very little. In the general election of 1900 they happily sent eighty-one Home Rule members to Westminster. But what little hope the Parliamentary Party had of a Home Rule measure disappeared when the Conservatives were elected for a second consecutive term.

Gerald Balfour, who as Chief Secretary had carried through the Land Act of 1896, had once remarked prophetically that it was not possible to 'kill Home Rule with kindness', but the Conservatives now attempted to do so. One major reform was the almost revolutionary Land Act of 1903, usually called the Wyndham Act after the brilliant but erratic Chief Secretary who managed to push it through and so end the land war. Again, even with an amending act in 1909, it did not go quite far enough and there was agitation of a minor kind. British politicians, for whom the land problem had loomed so large for so long, never quite ceased to think of the Irish people as militant peasants and never understood the aspirations they were so forcefully to make clear.

As yet, Griffith and Rooney had offered no constructive alternatives to the Home Rule policy of the Parliamentary Party, whose objectives seemed to them to encompass no more than the freedom to run Ireland as a British annexe. Griffith still regarded Rooney as his leader and, rather surprisingly, was himself often thought of as indolent. Both, in fact, were tireless, writing, lecturing and organising.

Griffith had been turning over in his mind for some time ways of bringing into a single homogeneous organisation the many groups which were seeking to halt

the anglicisation of Irish life and to advance the Irish
[20] language, Irish literature, Irish theatre, Irish games and, above all, an Irish government controlling Ireland's own industry, economy, education, culture and relations with other countries. In September 1900, he formed Cumann na nGaedheal, which met formally for the first time two months later. A kind of holdall, its objects were deliberately vague so that any appropriate organisation could be included. Yeats, who had taken part in the preliminary discussions, described the aim as: 'The rooting of the whole Irish people in Ireland, the weakening of every force and influence that tends to drive them into exile or makes them unworthy of their fathers while they remain at home.'[9] Griffith himself saw it as a loose federation of existing autonomous societies, as a forum.

At the November Convention he spoke brilliantly. 'I never did the like before,' he admitted.[10] Couched in trenchant language, the resolution he put forward demanded that the members of the Irish Parliamentary Party should refuse 'to attend the British parliament or recognise its right to legislate for Ireland', and should 'remain at home to help in promoting Ireland's interest and to aid in guarding its national rights'.[11]

Towards the end of the year, Griffith heard from John MacBride that he was coming to Paris. Griffith hastened to see him. Maud Gonne went too, and met her future husband. MacBride could not return to Ireland without being arrested and Griffith was concerned about his future. It was decided that a lecture tour of America was the answer and Griffith helped his friend put his experiences on paper. In America MacBride was joined by Maud Gonne. Griffith was one of many who warned them against marriage. Though both were dear friends, he foresaw unhappiness and, indeed, the two separated soon after the birth of their son Sean, who was destined to play a militant role in Irish affairs.

On 6 May 1901, William Rooney died at the age of twenty-seven. Griffith was desolate and for many weeks his pen recorded little but his grief. His family and Rooney's had lived in the same house, and scarcely a thought had entered his head that he had not shared with Rooney. Emotionally drained and intellectually alone, he wrote to Maud Gonne begging her not to stay too long in America. But the pain dulled and Griffith's confidence in himself returned. For some time at least, he must replace his lost leader. Looking back, Michael Collins saw Rooney rather than Griffith as the prophet. 'He prepared the way and foresaw the victory, and he helped his nation rise, and by developing its soul, to get ready for victory.'[12]

Soon the acid returned to Griffith's inkwell and he produced a series of articles under the heading of 'The Game of Humbug'. For Griffith the greatest humbug of all was the attendance of Irish representatives at Westminster. There was a stream of callers to his office at 17 Fownes Street, which P. S. O'Hegarty has described: 'The room, I should say, was small, with one grimy window, one table and two chairs, bound files of the *United Irishman* leaning against the wall, and papers everywhere, on the floor, on the one visitor's chair, all over the place. It had the peculiar masculine disorder which no woman understands, that is to say that its disorder was only apparent. He knew where to find everything. But it was without ornament or impedimenta of any kind, a working room, strictly conditioned to a task, like the man himself.'[13] Recalling his first meeting with Griffith in about 1912, General Richard Mulcahy commented that his office 'was small and cramped and showed the untidiness that is perhaps inevitably associated with such work'[14] – the puzzled but tolerant attitude of a man who could not himself bear untidiness.

Few people were on intimate terms with Griffith.
[22] He did not give his friendship easily, was difficult to work with, and quickly parted company with those who disagreed with him. After Rooney's death these traits were more evident.

Sean T. O'Kelly often went to Fownes Street to hand in manuscripts which, mostly unavailingly, he submitted to the editor of the *United Irishman.* On one occasion, in about 1902, he met Griffith on the stairs. Griffith recognised him as a helpful young assistant in the National Library and invited him to his office. A friendship developed which lasted, O'Kelly says, until they disagreed about the Treaty. He, Griffith and Henry Dixon met almost daily for lunch, at Mrs Wyse Power's Irish Farm Produce restaurant, from 1903 to 1916.[15]

Keen on physical fitness, Griffith walked or cycled at weekends and swam every morning. It was, O'Kelly surmises, at the 'Forty-Foot', a men's bathing place, that he met Oliver St John Gogarty, whose friendship he retained to the end of his life. Once, Gogarty challenged Griffith to swim with him across Dublin Bay from the Martello tower at Sandymount. They set off, but half way across Gogarty began to wonder whether the double crossing might prove too much for his friend. Pretending weariness, he turned back, taking the solicitous Griffith with him.[16]

Arthur Griffith continued to work hard but it was not until the third annual Convention of Cumann na nGaedheal that, his ideas having crystallised, he produced a policy, which he named the 'Hungarian policy', and to which, though it was often lampooned, he adhered with the immovability of a medieval wall. Upon its foundation Sinn Féin was constructed. He had studied the politics of central Europe and had been fascinated by the struggle of the Hungarians, led by Déak, to regain the sovereign status of their country.

He told the story and elaborated his arguments in a series of articles published first in the *United Irishman* and then in a pamphlet, 'The Resurrection of Hungary, A Parallel for Ireland', published in 1904.

The parallel was not meticulous. Austria had crushed the Hungarian revolt of 1848–9 and with it the republic established by Louis Kossuth. Defeated by the Italians shortly afterwards, Austria was hard pressed to keep her empire with its numerous ethnic minorities together. From 1860 she tried one constitutional experiment after another. 'The Magyars would no more come into a Parliament at Vienna to be voted down by Germans that Ulstermen would sit in a nationalist Parliament in Dublin'[17] is the ironical parallel suggested by one English historian. But that is hardly the way Griffith saw it.

Finally, the Austrian Emperor invited the Hungarians to put their proposals. Déak opposed secession but was determined to obtain political liberty for the Magyars. In 1867, Déak and the Austrian Chancellor Buest reached a settlement by which each country had independence but recognised the Emperor. The lesson Griffith tried to make clear to the Irish people was that the Hungarians had won their independence, not in the Diet of Vienna, but by refusing to send representatives there. Ireland's independence had to be won in Ireland, he insisted.

Withdrawal of Irish representatives from Westminster was no new idea. O'Connell and Parnell had both considered it. Thomas Davis had put it forward in 1844 and, in 1868, the year after the abortive Fenian rising, *The Irishman* had even anticipated Griffith by pointing to the example of Hungary. But no one had ever persevered with the idea as Griffith did. Year after year he plugged away at it, constantly refining his ideas of how an Irish government should function once it was established. 'Arthur Griffith was so stub-

born,' wrote George William Russell (AE), 'that I
[24] think he must, like Ulysses in the Platonic myth, have made up his mind before he was born and been unable to alter it afterwards.'[18]

Griffith adopted the dual monarchy concept, though he was essentially a separatist, partly because he believed it would work, but mostly because he knew that it offered the only chance of persuading the Ulster Protestants to accept an All-Ireland parliament. The machinery existed; because of the Renunciation Act of 1783 Britain had no right to legislate for Ireland; thus the Union was invalid and the Grattan constitution extant. When Griffith spoke of himself as a 'King, Lords and Commons man', as he sometimes did, he was referring to the King, Lords and Commons of Ireland. In this he was in direct descent from both Grattan and O'Connell. Speaking in the House of Commons in 1834, when he moved Repeal of the Union, Daniel O'Connell envisaged Ireland 'as another and distinct country, subject to the same King, but having a Legislature totally independent of the Legislature of Great Britain.'[19] Arthur Griffith might well have spoken those words himself.

Griffith had also pondered an economic policy for Ireland and had found inspiration in the German protectionist economist, Friedrich List. He wanted to build up Irish industry behind a tariff wall with funds withdrawn from British companies by Irish investors; he also had plans for reafforestation and for a merchant fleet.

In 1903 he formed yet another organisation, the National Council, whose principal aim, on a somewhat lower level than economic planning, was to organise protests against the visit to Ireland of Edward VII and Queen Alexandra. At a mass meeting of the United Irish League in the Rotunda, Griffith demanded to know whether or not the Lord Mayor intended to present a loyal address. Pressed, the Lord Mayor lost his temper and hurled a chair into the auditorium, surprising Griffith who always expected reasoned arguments. The meeting broke up but the campaign continued and in a close vote the Dublin Corporation decided against a loyal address. But the protesters were still a minority and the King made an almost triumphal progress through Ireland.

The National Council continued in existence and established itself in premises at 6 Harcourt Street. Griffith was inclined to see the Council rather than Cumann na nGaedheal as his political instrument, for the all-embracing nature of the latter prevented the emergence of a spearhead. Two young men in Belfast, Bulmer Hobson and Denis McCullough, both members of the IRB, were impatient of the seeming inactivity of both Cumann na nGaedheal and the National Council and formed the first Dungannon Club. They were soon joined by Patrick MacCartan who started a club in Dublin, and Sean MacDermott, who became a full-time organiser and formed clubs in various parts of the country. P. S. O'Hegarty took up the idea in London and George Gavan Duffy joined him.

The Dungannon Clubs specialised in anti-recruiting campaigns and the publication of illegal literature and covertly recruited for the IRB. Hobson was very active on platforms in England as well as in Ireland. His gospel fundamentally was that of Griffith but he disagreed on the issue of dual monarchy. The Dungannon Clubs advocated a republic. They 'did not see how complete independence could take any other form in Ireland'.[20]

So many leagues and clubs and councils had come into being that, like too many children in a bed, they were likely to suffocate each other. Taking the lead, at the annual convention of the National Council in

November 1905, Griffith propounded his policy once
[26] again, elaborating the detail and calling it the 'Sinn Féin' policy.

One day, at his office in Fownes Street, Griffith had been discussing his ideas with an enthusiastic member of the Gaelic League, Máire Butler. 'The policy of *Sinn Féin* in fact,' she said. '*Sinn Féin*,' he cried, 'are exactly the two words which express my meaning.'[21]

Sinn Féin! Ourselves! The expression distilled the very essence of the whole nationalist movement. But Griffith and Rooney had seen the appropriateness of it as far back as his sojourn in Africa and, as Colum suggests, they may have borrowed it unconsciously from some Irish verses written by Douglas Hyde which ended with the words *Sinn Féin amháin* – Ourselves alone.[22]

It was to this National Council audience, modest in size and already converted, that Griffith first mentioned List. Speaking confidently, he surveyed the state of Irish agriculture and industry, analysed its weaknesses, made constructive suggestions: incentives to farmers to till the land instead of fattening cattle for export to England; a balance between agriculture and industry to promote self-sufficiency; understanding between manufacturers and farmers who were inclined to think their respective interests were separate; protection, not to exclude foreign goods but to enable Irish industries to develop and Irish goods to compete on equal terms.

He put forward his ideas for afforestation and a merchant fleet; called for reforms in education, advocated Irish representatives in foreign countries, an Irish civil service and courts, and, taking a leaf from O'Connell's book, a Council of Three Hundred with a nucleus of abstentionist MPs, which would become a national *de facto* government. He envisaged also an upper house of recognised experts in various fields.

In April 1907, Cumann na nGaedheal and the Dungannon Clubs amalgamated as the Sinn Féin League. A few months earlier, in a letter to George Gavan Duffy, Bulmer Hobson had written: 'The National Council has no strength in Dublin – the C[umann] na nG[aedheal] and they are not pulling well – and altogether they seem to be a poor lot.' He thought that if there were to be a merger, the Constitution of 1782 should be no part of the policy. An executive should be formed of the twelve to fifteen best men from any part of the country. To a suggestion that he should meet with Griffith and Walter Cole, Hobson told Gavan Duffy, 'I am in your hands – do as you think best – but what if they preach '82 Renunciation Act etc. and I separatism – the only thing which I could honestly advocate.'[23] [27]

The meeting took place, with Denis McCullough as Hobson's fellow delegate, and, although Griffith and Cole would not accept conditions, the deal went through. In September 1908, the National Council also came into the alliance – Griffith being outvoted according to Hobson[24] – and there was now a single organisation, Sinn Féin.

'The Resurrection of Hungary' had sold 30,000 copies and if most of them had been bought by the converted, many also were purchased by the merely receptive. The young Richard Mulcahy, for one, bought the pamphlet the day it appeared and, years later, wrote that it was like 'a quiet blood-transfusion'.[25]

But not everyone was inspired. D. P. Moran, a caustic journalist, who had learned his trade in London and had founded his own paper, *The Leader*, in 1900, was one. Moran wanted an Ireland intellectually as well as politically independent. For him the patriotic ideal was too often parcelled up in pious rhetoric. He was scathing about the Irish Parliamentary Party, equally scornful of Sinn Féin. The 'Green Hungarian

Band,' he called it. He had much in common with
[28] Griffith and campaigned for protectionism by what amounted to a boycott of non-Irish goods. Like Hobson, he saw no merit in Grattan's Parliament and no point in Griffith's preoccupation with 1782.

At public meetings Hobson was continually challenged on Griffith's Hungarian parallel and eventually abandoned the analogy. The relevant question, parallel or not, was whether the policy was good for Ireland. Griffith was annoyed. 'He wanted his teaching to be accepted as a whole.'[26]

Early in 1907, responding to an invitation from John Devoy, the powerful Irish-American leader, Hobson sailed for America to explain Sinn Féin. Passing through Dublin, Hobson called on Griffith and 'was surprised at the coldness and hostility of his attitude.' It transpired that Griffith had already suggested he should be invited on a similar mission.[27] These incidents marked the beginning of an estrangement between the two men. There was no quarrel apparently, just the cooling towards one who did not agree with him, which was a weakness of Arthur Griffith.

In Hobson's view, Griffith had watered down his objectives and was no longer a separatist. To O'Hegarty, Griffith put the position as he saw it: 'I am a separatist. The Irish people are not separatists. I do not think that they can be united behind a separatist policy. But I do think that it is possible to unite them on this policy.'[28]

If Griffith was making a realistic appraisal of the Irish people as a whole, in the short term he had to make concessions in the wording of Sinn Féin's constitution to retain the support of young militants, especially those who had come in through the merger with the Dungannon Clubs. So from the outset there was an uneasy dichotomy and that was to persist.

The *United Irishman*, unable to pay damages for libel awarded against it, went out of business. Sinn Féin Printing and Publishing Company Ltd was formed and a new paper, *Sinn Féin*, appeared. Griffith's publishing ventures were always beset by financial problems. The accounts for the financial year ended 27 April 1907 disclose expenditure of £1,251. 19. 9, of which £185. 18. 0 was paid for salaries and wages. Income amounted to £1,123. 14. 9 and there was therefore a loss of £128. 5. 0.[29] Little wonder that Arthur Griffith, who had become engaged to Maud Sheehan in 1904, had to wait until 1910 to marry her.

His future wife was not much interested in his political activities. The bond between them was music. Somehow he still found time for musical evenings at the Sheehans' home and to sustain their courtship. He also found relaxation at the home of a Protestant family named Williams. The three daughters, Lily, Nora and Flo, were to become ardent supporters. His letters to them from prison in years to come reveal a man different from the pugnacious, often taciturn Griffith of the political arena. Lily was a talented painter. Griffith seemed drawn to creative artists, yet he reproached Edward Martyn for giving £10,000 to found a choir instead of financing a newspaper to promote the nationalist cause. Perhaps the miserable living he eked out from his work explains his covetousness.

His quarrel with Yeats is less understandable. Intensely moved by *Cathleen ni Houlihan*, written for Maud Gonne and produced in a small hall in 1902, he condemned J. M. Synge's *In the Shadow of the Glen* when it was performed by the Irish Literary Theatre the following year. Synge had broken with tradition, creating a real life drama but using English in a way which echoed the cadences of Irish speech.

But his heroine, the lonely girl-wife of an elderly man,
[30] deserted him for another man, a theme which inevitably offended Catholics and provoked Griffith into protesting that no Irish woman could so transgress. This prudish streak surfaced again a few years later when he criticised Lloyd George for making unmarried mothers eligible to receive a child allowance. This, declared Griffith, was 'to tax the married woman to support immorality'.[30]

But the issue was broader. It was not only a question of affronted religious faith but of what an artist owed to a cause, in this case, Irish-Ireland. Griffith summed up the argument of one side with the words: 'If the Irish theatre ceases to reflect Irish life and embody Irish aspiration the world will wag its head away from it.' In reply, Yeats asserted that literature was 'always one man's vision of the world', and warned: 'A community that is opinion-ridden, even when those opinions are in themselves noble, is likely to put its creative minds into some sort of prison.'[31]

Wound into the argument of art as individual expression or art as the pulse of a people, was the filament of language. There were those who would be content with nothing less than the whole of Irish literature appearing in the Irish language. Turning on Yeats, Maud Gonne wrote, 'Mr Yeats asks for freedom for the theatre, freedom even from patriotic activity. I would ask for freedom for it from one thing more deadly than all else – freedom from the insidious and destructive tyranny of foreign influence.'[32] Griffith was too realistic to go as far as that. Works in Irish were appearing, notably by Douglas Hyde, but they were likely to be few and far between for a very long time. Yeats and Synge were trying to create a body of modern Irish literature. That the language was English was unavoidable. It was the spirit of the writing and the subject matter with which Griffith quarrelled.

In the clash between the two traditions, that of ancient, historic Ireland and that which had transcended it, [31]
Griffith upheld the one and made use of the other.

The irony is that Irish writers from Dean Swift to Beckett have given the English language an unmistakably Irish sheen. In the hands of an Irish writer English becomes an Irish language, rich and vital.

Synge aroused further controversy with *The Playboy of the Western World* in 1907 and Griffith was again in the van of the critics. He had little now to do with Yeats, who more or less abandoned the nationalism of his youth but, going his own way, still contributed his huge talent to the cause.

3
Irish Stew

Few Irish people concerned themselves with the intellectual quarrels of the articulate minority. Although the majority favoured self-government, they were content to wait patiently for the Parliamentary Party to produce it in the course of time. The poor and ill-educated were too hard-pressed to worry about political theories or the glories of long ago.

In the British general election of January 1906, the Liberals had a landslide win and didn't need the support of the Irish Parliamentary Party. But they were at the mercy of the House of Lords, where the Conservative-Unionists were only too eager to redress the balance in the Commons by blocking Liberal measures for reform. The omens for Home Rule, therefore, were not good. Furthermore, many of the Liberals were tired of the Irish Question. Rather apologetically, the Prime Minister, Sir Henry Campbell-Bannerman, introduced in 1907 the Irish Council Bill. It offered, if not a step, a slight shuffle towards self-government. In Ireland there was disappointment and anger and Redmond, now firmly in the driving seat of the Parliamentary Party, denounced the measure. The government had little option but to drop it.

Urged by Griffith, some members of Redmond's party advocated withdrawal from Westminster. Three resigned and one, C. J. Dolan, actually resigned his North Leitrim seat and offered to stand at the by-election as a Sinn Féin candidate, declining to take the seat if he won. Sinn Féin was not geared for electioneering but this was a challenge Griffith could not possibly resist if Sinn Féin was to retain any credibility. Dolan was soundly beaten by the Parliamentary Party's new candidate but a point had been made and Griffith seized upon it: 'From the day the representatives of Ireland first crossed the sea to sit in an Alien Parliament and lend its acts sanction by their presence – that fatal January 1st, 1801 – until Friday last, no vote has been cast in an election in Ireland in denial of the authority of that Parliament to rule Ireland.'[1]

The episode demonstrated the impotence of the Parliamentary Party when they could bring no leverage against the Liberals who, however, were not altogether blinkered and continued to introduce legislation to improve Irish conditions. Working-class housing was one area of need to benefit and there was some tidying-up of the Wyndham Act, but the legislation of most interest to Sinn Féin and other nationalist groups was the Universities Act of 1908, which appeared to bring to an end almost a century of fierce in-fighting with both political and religious difference at the core of it.

Of the three 'Queen's' Colleges, in Belfast, Galway and Cork, established by Sir Robert Peel in 1845 and dismissed by O'Connell as 'godless' because, in theory at least, they were undenominational, Belfast was given university status and Cork and Galway became, with the Jesuit College in Dublin, constituent colleges in a new National University. Griffith would have wished Dublin University to have a second college, to cater for Catholic students. Trinity, the University's one existing college, was not enthusiastic and succeeded in remaining outside the new provisions. It had been declared 'a satisfactory organ for the higher education of the Protestant Episcopal population of Ireland'. Griffith disagreed, alleging that it had 'wilfully hidden the truth from our Protestant fellow countrymen,

and taught them instead that from the Irish nation
[34] they derive no rights, and to it they owe no duties'.[2]

Nationalist organisations generally took the view that the creation of the new university would further their cause. Griffith wanted the emphasis to be on teaching 'which will give us captains of industry, doctors of agriculture, and men of science – men skilled to lead the nation in its fight for material existence'.[3]

For the Gaelic Leaguers the cardinal requirement was that the Irish language be taught, not as an end in itself but, as they had always argued, as a means of restoring to Ireland her own culture. The scholarly Eoin Mac Néill put the case succinctly in a pamphlet: 'The basis of higher education in Ireland ought to be distinctively Irish, not English or Cosmopolitan,' was his premise. The Irish language was the one factor which could confer this distinctive Irishness, and therefore a knowledge of Irish should be a requirement for matriculation and in non-specialised courses. There was opposition from the Catholic hierarchy and from some political leaders. Griffith, who had once held that the Irish language was not essential to an Irish nationality, vigorously supported Mac Néill and Hyde. The cause was won when the majority of county councils, given powers to award scholarships, agreed that Irish should be a requirement.

Later, in 1913, Griffith and Hyde quarrelled over what Hyde called 'the University fight'. Replying to a letter Griffith had written and published, Hyde wrote,[4] 'Your letter consists of assertions and I deny every one of them.' The campaign for the Irish language to be a required subject in the National University had been won, Hyde declared, by a resolution of the National Convention under Redmond and the action of the county councils in promising scholarships only if Irish was essential. 'But who addressed the National Convention and who stirred up the County

Councils?' asked Hyde, and went on: 'If you imagine, as I think you modestly suggest, that it was your paper which won the fight for essential Irish (I suppose by bringing round the County Councils and the National Convention, of which last you say nothing), then I am afraid I disagree with you, for I don't think the bulk of the participants had the advantage of being readers of *Sinn Féin*.'

Arthur Griffith had long wanted to make *Sinn Féin* into a daily newspaper. The effectiveness of the daily press in the North Leitrim by-election sharpened his resolve but, its funds depleted by electioneering expenses, the Sinn Féin executive was reluctant to risk the enterprise. Griffith stubbornly raised enough funds from all sources – about £4,000 of £8,000 required[5] to put the paper on a sound footing – to launch it but not to sustain its life beyond a few months.

The finances of *Sinn Féin* were a constant worry and Griffith regretted he could not pay his contributors more. James Stephens, who began his literary career with *Sinn Féin* and became Griffith's friend, noted that 'Yeats and Russell, Colum, O'Sullivan, Connolly, Alice Milligan, with Oliver Gogarty as a kind of perpetually disappearing astonishment, all wrote for him.'[6] As Griffith and Stephens walked home one evening, Griffith lamented that he hadn't a streak of dishonesty in his makeup. Otherwise, he could have been wealthy himself and paid his contributors more. As he was talking, three young men tried to pick a fight with them. There was a fracas which ended when the police arrived. Declining to charge his assailants, Griffith resumed his monologue about the unfortunate consequences of his rectitude.

Griffith enjoyed a joke and could laugh 'as heartily as a bull', Stephens says, but 'the joke of a literary friend was as sacred to him as any other man's raw material was . . .' He had a sly humour of his own. On one occasion a Castle circular warning staff to avoid talking too much to 'the man in the street' came into his hands. Griffith printed it, adding a note that the street referred to was Fownes Street.

Stephens regarded him as 'the greatest journalist working in the English tongue'. He could tackle almost any subject and often, when contributors failed to meet a deadline, would write their articles himself. In a letter to James Starkey, better known as Seamus O'Sullivan, in which he asked him to review an art exhibition, Griffith wrote: 'Now I can admire and appreciate good pictures, but I know too little of the subject to criticise them with any confidence.' He added that, if need be, he would 'muddle through'.[7]

O'Sullivan was introduced to the *United Irishman* by George Russell ('AE') who told him it was 'the only Irish weekly worth buying', but it was Padraic Colum who first took O'Sullivan up the rickety stairs at Fownes Street to meet Griffith himself. O'Sullivan's first impression[8] was of a man 'low-sized' but whose 'broad shoulders suggested immense strength', and whose 'well-set jawbone' lent him a 'stern, even belligerent expression'. He was struck by the 'innate and unconquerable shyness' of the man, whose close friend he became. Together they haunted the Dublin book-carts on Saturday afternoons and O'Sullivan was shocked 'when my friend, Arthur Griffith, confided to me, on one of those Saturday afternoon outings which he so enjoyed, that the most valuable contributions on financial subjects which he had published in his paper were the work of a North of Ireland Orange leader'.[9]

Sinn Féin ran as an evening paper from 24 August 1909 to 22 January 1910 and might well have paid its way had Griffith's capital not run out. John Sweetman, a retired Catholic businessman who had financed publication of 'The Resurrection of Hungary' and later became President of Sinn Féin, wrote to George Gavan Duffy: 'I hear the funds of the Sinn Féin daily newspaper are nearly exhausted. I did not subscribe to it at first, as I did not believe that sufficient funds could be obtained and I did not wish to encourage its starting.'[10] He had sent £200 to prolong the life of the paper. 'Besides the good it directly does through its readers, it is having an effect on the other newspapers and perhaps persons of all political parties might very well subscribe to it for the purpose of keeping it going.'

Sweetman's reference to other political groups was well informed. In 1907, before the North Leitrim by-election, William O'Brien, one-time anti-Parnellite and a perpetual thorn in Redmond's side, had proposed a conference in which he wanted Sinn Féin to join. The idea had come to nothing then, but in March 1909, O'Brien made a further approach. His aim was to bring together, through his All-for-Ireland League, all but the extremists in both the Unionist and Parliamentary camps. Adversaries at one time, O'Brien and Griffith had quite a lot in common. Griffith had in any case become more tolerant of those whose views differed from his. But his price for joint action with the All-for-Ireland League – a resolution demanding withdrawal from Westminster – was too much for O'Brien.[11]

On 9 December 1909, James Brady, O'Brien's solicitor and a Sinn Féin member of Dublin Corporation, wrote to George Gavan Duffy[12] floating the idea that Sinn Féin might 'admit parliamentary representatives on certain conditions' and suggesting that he and Gavan Duffy stand for Dublin constituencies in the general election of January 1910. Behind the idea, which threatened to up-end the platform on which Griffith had stood for so many years, was that after the election the Irish Parliamentary Party might

well hold the balance of power in the House of Com-
[38] mons and Sinn Féin would be left high and dry. After
long, ineffectual years, a new sweep of the road to
freedom had opened up before the parliamentarians.

Lloyd George's 1909 budget was as unpopular in Ireland as it was in Britain. The Lords threatened to veto it. The Parliamentary Party faced a dilemma. If they supported the budget they would themselves court unpopularity in Ireland. On the other hand, there was an opportunity to put pressure on the Liberals. The House of Lords, with whom the Liberals had been scrapping throughout the life of the parliament, was the real barrier to Home Rule. Redmond decided to support the Liberals in return for an undertaking that the Lords' power of veto would be curtailed. The Liberals were not very amenable to pressure of this kind but the Lords themselves drastically changed the whole situation by throwing out the budget. The Liberals had no option but to go to the country.

The Brady proposals came before the Sinn Féin executive on 20 December and caused ructions between moderates and republicans. For the moderates the concept of abstention from Westminster seemed much less attractive and a highly impracticable compromise was mooted. Elected members might attend at Westminster as delegates on relevant occasions but they would not be considered representatives. This was thrown out but not before Countess Markiewicz and other republicans had tried to bait Griffith into an admission that he approved the compromise. Griffith, trying to be impartial, favoured rejection of the Brady proposals but was not against listening to the ideas of other groups. For months the controversy rumbled on in the belly of the Sinn Féin movement as people tried to work out ways of climbing on the Redmond bandwaggon without abandoning their own.

Redmond now had the whip hand. There were, in

the event, two general elections in 1910, negotiations between the Conservative-Unionists and the Liberals to try to break the deadlock having failed. The results differed little. At the final count the two main parties each had 273 seats, Labour had forty-two, Redmond's party had seventy-three and there were ten Irish independents. The first issue was the House of Lords, and the peers, threatened by the creation of a body of new peers, to which the King, George V, agreed, gave way. The Parliament Act of 1911 removed their right to veto finance bills altogether and provided that other legislation could be rejected twice only in successive years.

Arthur Griffith was not the man to stand in Redmond's way. His own convictions were unchanged but he was ready to accept a Home Rule measure as a stepping-stone to a free and independent Ireland. With staunch supporters such as Sean Milroy, he set about putting Sinn Féin's house in order, mainly by centralising the handful of branches which remained. For the movement dwindled rapidly, losing both moderates, who transferred their allegiance to the Parliamentary Party, and republicans like Bulmer Hobson, McCullough and MacCartan who, if nothing else, were weary of committee meetings and sceptical of Griffith's capacity to achieve more than he had already. This, they recognised, was inestimable. No man had done more than he to create and foster the resurgent nationalism of which they were part. But Sinn Féin had its faithful adherents among those who looked beyond Home Rule and Griffith himself was quietly confident that within fifteen years the Sinn Féin ideal would have been realised.

His was a full life. As well as keeping his paper going week in, week out, he spent long hours writing alone; there were innumerable committee meetings and lectures, a massive correspondence and meetings with his

cronies at the Bailey. Yet he found time for physical
[40] recreation, more musical evenings at the Misses Williams', for concerts and oratorio – his attendance at which was a constant surprise to his friends. They were surprised, too, when on 24 November 1910, the long engagement to Maud Sheehan ended with their wedding at the church of St John the Baptist, Clontarf. Griffith was now thirty-nine. Mrs Griffith, who had waited so long, was to enjoy but twelve years of intermittent companionship while her husband was carried in the swirl of events of a momentous decade. They lived in Clontarf, in a house given to them by friends, and subsisted on Griffith's meagre earnings. In September 1911, a son, Nevin, was born to Mrs Griffith. Her husband's pleasure is evident in the letter he wrote to the Williams sisters to explain why he had not kept an appointment. It was, he wrote, 'owing to the unexpected arrival of a stranger in my house – a youth whom neither my wife or myself expected for another fortnight.'[13] About eighteen months later, their daughter, Ita, was born.

In 1911, Sweetman having resigned, Griffith became President of Sinn Féin. He did not regret its eclipse as a political party, for he had never set out to build one. The growth of branches and clubs had been inspired by his more militant followers. His mission had always been to educate public opinion through his own newspaper, to work with words. He was an enabler rather than a leader. He had produced a policy which he believed would work for Ireland and he had set out to create the climate in which it could work. Now that he had no longer to try to hold together dissident groups, had no longer responsibility for numerous branches throughout the country, he had reverted to his role of nearly a decade before. He was once more primarily an educational campaigner. Militant colleagues such as Bulmer Hobson and McCullough were active in other directions. Hobson was now editor of *Irish Freedom*, which was controlled by the IRB, now quietly and quickly expanding.

Dominated at the beginning of the century by old Fenians whose fervour was undiminished but whose energies time had sapped, the IRB had seemed a spent force. Re-organised in 1907, it was a tighter, tauter organisation. Gradually, the dead wood at the top was removed, new entrants were screened to prevent the all-too-frequent incursions by British agents, and the Supreme Council adopted the policy of infiltrating other organisations. The aim was to have members in positions where they could be useful when the time came. Ordinary members of the IRB had little idea of what was going on. The activity was all at the top. Richard Mulcahy 'never found the IRB to be anything but a monthly roll-call'.[14] But when the Volunteers came into being in 1913, IRB members were instructed: 'Join the Volunteers and take your orders from your superior officers.' Because the IRB was carefully choosing its members, seeking intelligent, well-educated young men from the Gaelic League, Sinn Féin, the Gaelic Athletic Association and kindred groups, those superior officers were likely to be IRB men.

Many of the members took the IRB oath in the little newsagent's and tobacconist's shop established by Tom Clarke on his return from America in 1907. Clarke, who had been released from prison in 1898 after serving fifteen brutal years for his part in a dynamite campaign in the early 1880s, was a fanatical Irish patriot. It was to him that the young activists of the IRB looked for leadership.

Clarke had been an absentee vice-president of Cumann na nGaedheal and Arthur Griffith was a frequent visitor to his shop, though Griffith had left the IRB, probably in 1910 but possibly earlier, because the oath inhibited his independence as leader of a political movement. During his nine years in America Clarke had worked with Clan na Gael and it may have been he, as earlier it had been John MacBride, that persuaded Clan na Gael to help Griffith's *Sinn Féin* through its stickier financial patches. For even as Sinn Féin declined, the IRB recognised that it still had a political structure, a philosophy and a programme which the IRB itself would need.

Most of the men who were to become household names in the next few years were as yet little known, but they were gathering in the wings as the well tried performers took the stage.

Herbert Asquith, Prime Minister and leader of the Liberals since Campbell-Bannerman's death in 1908, had never shown much enthusiasm for Home Rule. He had once declared, too, that his party should not try to form a government if they had to rely on the support of Irish members, but he had needed their support to get the 1909 budget through and to deal with the vexed problem of the powers of the House of Lords. Now, to stay in power, he had no option but to introduce the third Home Rule Bill, which he did, phlegmatically, in 1912. With the Lords ultimately powerless to prevent it, Redmond seemed to have all the cards in his hand. But there was one, Randolph Churchill's famous Orange Card, which was yet to be played.

The removal of the Lords veto had brought joy into the Nationalist camp but the Unionists had taken fright and, as always in times of crisis, the occasion produced the man. The Unionists had not been a force in Irish politics until 1885 when Gladstone's first Home Rule Bill, defeated in the following year, became a threat to the Union. Their advent was to deepen the divisions, which had long existed in Ireland, between Catholic and Protestant. The resultant polarisation had virtually wiped out Liberalism in Ireland, as it also prevented Labour from making any headway, leaving the Nationalists and the Unionists, overwhelmingly Catholic and Protestant, respectively, as the protagonists.

Of vital importance, too, was the resurgence in Ulster of the Orange Order, the militant Protestant Order founded in 1795 and formally, though not entirely, disbanded in 1836. The Order was not designed to fulfil the role of a political party, though its members included men of high position and power. Blatantly propagandist, it was adept at rousing the emotions of the masses. The Orangemen, desperately anxious to preserve the Union, lent their support to various attempts made over the next years to build up a political party. The most effective was the Ulster Unionist Council formed in 1905. In the South, the Irish Unionist Alliance had only a few hundred members. They were from the wealthy land-owning class, many with British interests and family connections. Leaving parliamentary action to the North, they undertook, under the aegis of a joint committee of Unionist associations, most of the propaganda against Asquith's Home Rule Bill.

The man whom the hour produced was Edward Carson, elected to parliament in 1892 as a Liberal Unionist for Dublin University – Trinity College. Solicitor-General in the last Conservative government, he was probably the most distinguished advocate of the day. In 1910, at the age of fifty-six, he was elected leader of the Irish Unionist group in parliament. A lanky, rather cadaverous looking man, he had dark hair, hooded eyes and a mouth twisted into a permanent sneer by the scepticism of years of cross-examining witnesses. He had the histrionic gifts of the barristers of his era and effortlessly held large audiences in thrall. Though much maligned, he was also admired by his adversaries. He believed utterly that it would be wrong

for Ireland to be a separate country and his motives
[44] were a good deal purer than those of many Ulster
Unionists in whose camp he inevitably found himself.

Even before the Home Rule Bill was introduced in April 1912, the Ulster Unionists prepared for battle. With his able lieutenant, James Craig, and others, Carson drew up a constitution for a provisional government of Ulster. Andrew Bonar Law, the new Conservative Party leader, a Canadian of Ulster stock, threw his authority behind Carson and the Ulster Unionists and preached something very close to treason.

Asquith's bill was hardly one to set the Liffey on fire. Ireland was to have her own parliament to regulate internal affairs, but the British government was to retain control of the purse strings and for that reason, and because she would be required to contribute to the defence budget, Ireland was still to have representation at Westminster. There were other reservations. Matters of defence, peace or war would also be in the hands of the British government, and for the time being they would also control the police.

Griffith wrote in *Sinn Féin:* 'If the Bill becomes law it will alter many Irish aspects, but it will alter no Irish ideals.' He was critical of the measure for it seemed to him that it would give Ireland no more than provincial status; but because he realised that the majority of Irish people supported it he took a neutral stance. He was convinced that the younger generation would not be satisfied, would demand more and would turn to Sinn Féin. So he did not oppose the Asquith bill but set his sights on the further goal, constantly reminding the people, especially young people, that until Ireland possessed fiscal powers, her own army, her own flag and her own foreign policy, real independence would not have been achieved. He had reason to be confident for it seemed to be accepted on all sides that it was no more than a provisional measure.

Provisional or not, it was anathema to the Ulster Unionists. James Craig, an effective but little known backbencher until the campaign against Home Rule, was a born organiser of boundless energy. Having persuaded Carson to accept the leadership,[15] he was content to work behind the scenes. He masterminded the theatrical signing of the Solemn League and Covenant on 28 September 1912, a tremendous protest demonstration with bands and banners whipping up the emotions. He was involved in the formation of the Ulster Volunteer Force and largely responsible for developing it into a formidable private army of 90,000 men with arms landed in a dramatic gun-running exploit in April 1914.

In Dublin, the lessons provided by Carson and Craig were quickly learned. On 25 November 1913, at the Rotunda in Dublin, Eoin Mac Néill, backed – though he was not aware of it – by the IRB, proposed the formation of a force of volunteers 'to secure and maintain the rights and liberties common to all the people in Ireland'.

Although he himself had not been invited to take part in the planning of the organisation, to which it was desired no political labels should be attached, Griffith saw the formation of the Volunteers as of immense importance. 'A national army strong enough to hold Ireland for the Irish may eventually be evolved,' he predicted. Redmond, on the verge of political success, demanded a share in the control of the Volunteers and got his way. At first, the enthusiastic recruits drilled with broom handles but in the following July they emulated the Ulster Volunteers' gun-running achievement, when arms were landed at Howth, a fishing village on the northern edge of Dublin Bay.

The autumn of 1913 had seen another conflict develop. For many thousands of workers in Dublin, miserably paid and living in awful slums, the Home Rule issue had little relevance. Unemployment was rife, hunger and disease commonplace. Two very remarkable men, James Larkin and James Connolly, were determined to improve their lot. Arriving in Dublin in 1908, after a period in Belfast, the fiery Larkin founded the Irish Transport and General Workers' Union. Connolly, who had returned to Ireland from America in 1910, became District Organiser of the union in Belfast. Griffith had never agreed with Connolly's socialism, although he liked the man. He regarded Larkin as an English trade unionist agitator and instigator of class warfare, whose activities were damaging industry and creating unemployment. Griffith had his own ideas about capital and labour which he saw as complementary to each other. 'The incentive and right of both is the profit of production,' he wrote,[16] 'and the security of one and the efficiency of the other are essential to national prosperity. . . .' It was the duty of an organised nation to protect labour and to ensure that the worker was justly remunerated. Sinn Féin would not 'associate itself with any war of classes'. Marxism he dismissed as 'neo-feudalism'.

The gibe at Marxism was directed at Connolly, like Griffith a considerable writer and polemicist. Whereas Griffith's concern was to use Ireland's resources so that wealth filtered down through the whole community, which retained its capitalist structure, Connolly saw the control of wealth vested in the working class. Larkin wanted to attack Britain on both the political and economic fronts and Connolly gradually came to share his view. Larkin's union, now with its own headquarters at Liberty Hall, grew rapidly in 1911 and 1912 as, capitalising on labour unrest in Britain, he used the sympathetic strike to achieve better wages and conditions in Ireland. He virtually controlled Ireland's ports.

In August 1913, he called tramway men out on strike. The employers retaliated by locking out members [47] of Larkin's union. The dispute, which went bitterly on into 1914 and caused destitution and misery, ended as the British trade union movement, fearful of being drawn into the dangerous Irish imbroglio, withdrew financial support. Larkin departed for America and Connolly took over. From the dispute a new force had emerged. This was the Citizen Army, brainchild of Captain Jack White VC, formed from the locked out workers, partly to occupy their time, partly to enable them to show some kind of cohesion in clashes with the police. The small force, which drilled at Liberty Hall, dwindled when the dispute faded but was revived by Sean O'Casey.

There were now a good many ingredients in the Irish stew, which showed every sign of boiling over into civil war in Ireland and in England. In May 1914, the Home Rule Bill passed through the Commons for the third time. The Lords now were powerless. But in Ulster Carson and Craig already had their plans for a provisional government and a well-disciplined, well-equipped army to back it. At the Curragh, British army officers had threatened to resign if ordered to move against Ulster. In Westminster, political opponents were not on speaking terms. King George V complained: 'The Government is drifting and taking me with it.' In July, he called a conference of the government and opposition, the Unionists and the Nationalists at Buckingham Palace. The conference failed. But now a new facet of the extraordinary prism had revealed itself. At first, no one had taken very seriously an amendment to the bill moved by T. G. R. Agar-Robartes. This was to exclude from its operation four Ulster counties. 'The stern fact we have to look in the face,' wrote Griffith, 'is that Ireland cannot acquiesce in any partition of her territory without

forfeiting all her rights as a nation'.[17] Suddenly the
[48] whole controversy ended and the threat of civil war vanished as Britain went to war with Germany. The Home Rule Act received royal assent, but its operation was suspended for twelve months or the duration of the war.

The majority of Irish people had accepted the Home Rule Act as a big step forward and were resigned to its postponement. No one thought the war would last very long in any case. But for the separatist movement the Act offered too little and had come too late. In 1912, Patrick Pearse had publicly supported the bill. A year later, he joined the IRB in Tom Clarke's shop and Clarke marked him out as a future leader.

It was Clarke who convened a meeting of people 'representative of advanced national opinion' to consider how to take advantage of Britain's preoccupation with Europe. The meeting was held in the library of the Gaelic League's headquarters in Parnell Square. Pearse, Connolly and Griffith were among those present and the possibility of a rising was mooted. It was an opportunity for the IRB to sound out opinion but they kept their own counsel. Perhaps as a cover, the Irish Neutrality League was formed to discourage recruiting to the British Army, but its public meetings were soon banned.

Redmond now enthusiastically offered the services of the Volunteers as a home guard in Ireland to release British personnel, an offer spurned by Kitchener. Griffith's reaction was characteristic: 'England is at war with Germany and Mr Redmond has offered England the services of the National Volunteers "to defend Ireland". What has Ireland to defend and whom has she to defend it against?' He urged the British government to withdraw 'the present abortive Home Rule Bill' and to pass 'a full measure of Home Rule'. Only then would Irishmen have 'some reason to

mobilise for the defence of their institutions'.[18] He suggested a rather startling alternative to Home Rule [49]
– a provisional government in Dublin set up by Redmond and Carson. 'Germany is nothing to us in herself,' wrote Griffith, 'but she is not our enemy. Our blood and our miseries are not on her head.'

Redmond did not share Griffith's neutrality and in a famous speech, at Woodenbridge in Co. Wicklow, he urged the Volunteers to fight for Britain anywhere. This split the Volunteer movement. The majority followed Redmond to form the National Volunteers; a quite small minority was reconstituted as the Irish Volunteers under a General Council with a central executive of nine members. Mac Néill was chief of staff; under him were three young men, Pearse, MacDonagh and Joseph Plunkett, who owed allegiance to the secret IRB. All were poets steeped in the Gaelic tradition. Unknown to Mac Néill, they were already planning insurrection.

In his publication, *Workers' Republic*, James Connolly openly advocated insurrection and the IRB conclave became anxious lest he lead his Citizen Army into a premature attack on the British. The ordinary rank and file of Volunteers, even those who were IRB members, had no inkling of what was afoot, nor did Arthur Griffith, who had joined the Volunteers and had carried a rifle at the Howth gun-running.

At the end of 1914, *Sinn Féin* was suppressed, together with *Irish Freedom* and other publications. Griffith hit on an ingenious ruse. Using cuttings from British and neutral publications, he managed to produce another paper, *Scissors and Paste*, which bore his unmistakable stamp. Within two months it too was banned. For a short time he had no livelihood; then he was asked to edit *Nationality*, financed by the IRB. It was agreed that he should be informed of any action contemplated by the IRB, the liaison

being the paper's business manager, Sean MacDermott,
 once organiser of the Dungannon Clubs and later of Sinn Féin branches. Griffith's views had not changed. In his heart he was a republican, but he still clung to the hope that there need be no partition of Ireland. The price of that, he believed, was continued attachment to the Crown. He was still convinced, too, that physical force was not the answer.

For that reason, perhaps, despite the agreement, he was kept in the dark by the IRB. When the old Fenian, O'Donovan Rossa, was buried at Glasnevin in August 1915, Pearse gave an oration at the graveside into which Griffith might have read more than he evidently did. And one may wonder that he was not alerted by certain of Pearse's writings. For Pearse the first sixteen months of the war were 'the most glorious in the history of Europe'.[19] He wrote of the 'august homage' to God, 'the homage of millions of lives given gladly for love of country. . . .' And Ireland? 'Ireland has not known the exhilaration of war for over a hundred years,' he wrote. He saw himself as a Christ figure dying that Ireland should be resurrected. The rational Arthur Griffith could only have dismissed as hyperbole this fantasia of Pearse.

The Supreme Council of the IRB had decided in the first month of the war to take advantage of England's preoccupation in Europe, but the initiative came from the Fenian organisation Clan na Gael in America, which had already been in touch with the Germans to sound out the possibility of military assistance. Sir Roger Casement was caught up in this intrigue when he arrived in America to seek funds for the Volunteers, of which he was treasurer. Financed by Clan na Gael, he went at once to Germany. He failed signally to recruit an Irish Brigade from prisoners of war, but did obtain a promise of arms and ammunition and of recognition of an independent Irish government if it could be won. Thereafter, Casement was little needed. Not he, but Joseph Plunkett, who travelled to Germany specially in the spring of 1915, arranged the shipment of arms needed for the insurrection planned for the following year.

In May 1915, the IRB set up a military committee, or Military Council, as it was later named, comprising Pearse, Plunkett, Eamonn Ceannt, Thomas Clarke and Sean MacDermott. Later in the year, unable to persuade Mac Néill that the Volunteers and the Citizen Army should join forces in an insurrection, James Connolly seemed hell-bent on leading his well-drilled but tiny Citizen Army into action. In January 1916, the Military Council was driven to confide in him. Connolly was sworn into the IRB and became a member of the Council. Shortly afterwards, Thomas MacDonagh became the seventh member of the Council. This group planned the Rising of Easter 1916. They went to extraordinary lengths to keep their plans secret, even from Mac Néill, who persistently questioned them.

Mac Néill wanted to build up the Volunteers so that Ireland could negotiate self-determination from a position of strength. He was ready to fight only if the British attempted either to disarm them or to impose conscription. If self-determination could be achieved by peaceful means, he saw no point in spilling blood. He had not yet appreciated that Pearse and his coterie were obsessed with the concept of a blood sacrifice.

In his courageous, posthumously published article in *Studies*, Father Shaw wrote that Mac Néill 'was speaking for the vast majority of Irish people' who 'generally had plainly chosen the broad constitutional mode of attaining national objectives'.

Even members of the IRB's Supreme Council had but a hazy idea of the plan and no idea of the date.

Certain Volunteer officers, who were IRB members,
[52] had instructions about the transportation of arms from Fenit, Co. Kerry where the *Aud*, which left Lubeck on 9 April, was to land them. Other officers, too, had been given some idea of what was expected of them; in general, orders had not been filtered down through the chain of command which was an essential part of the IRB's structure. In the event, there was confusion. There was confusion, too, over the arrival of the *Aud.* Arrangements with the Germans had had to be made through America. Mistakes were made which could not be rectified and the British, who had cracked the German code, were waiting for the vessel.

Rumours of the impending arrest of Sinn Féin and Volunteer leaders were given substance when Joseph Plunkett published what purported to be a detailed plan of the proposed round-up. Known as the 'Castle Document', it engendered great indignation and even Mac Néill was ready to fight until the authenticity of the document was questioned. It was a forgery, though it may have had a germ of truth, but it succeeded in heightening tension and inducing a belligerent mood among the Volunteers who, as yet, had no idea that belligerence was expected of them. They knew only that a full turn-out for manoeuvres on Easter Sunday had been organised.

The *Aud* arrived too soon, hung around the Kerry coast throughout Thursday night, and was intercepted by the British Navy on Good Friday, 21 April. Ordered into Queenstown Harbour, the German Captain scuttled his ship. Casement, with two companions, Robert Monteith and Daniel Bailey, landed from a submarine. Ironically, Casement's intention was to persuade the leaders against the insurrection. He was captured on Good Friday.

4
The Easter Rising

Sean T. O'Kelly relates[1] that he learned of the debacle of the *Aud* and of Casement's arrest from a *Freeman's Journal* reporter, J. F. O'Sullivan, and passed on the news to Arthur Griffith whom he met by chance. Griffith, O'Kelly says, was 'sore and vocal' about the IRB's failure to keep him informed.

Together they called on Mac Néill who, it transpired, had already learned about Casement and the *Aud.* Mac Néill revealed that he had known nothing of the IRB's plans for a rising on Easter Sunday until the early hours of Good Friday when he had been roused from his bed by Bulmer Hobson and J. J. ('Ginger') O'Connell. Having confronted Pearse, who claimed deception had been necessary, he had given orders to frustrate what he saw as an act of aggression. Later in the day, MacDermott and MacDonagh informed Mac Néill of the imminent arrival of the *Aud* and its arms cargo and persuaded him to withdraw.

Mac Néill half-decided to resign as Chief of Staff but, when news of the *Aud*'s scuttling reached him, he again cancelled the manoeuvres. His order was carried in the Sunday newspapers. This prevented any activity on the Sunday and ensured that throughout most of the country plans for a rising were put away. It also threw the Castle off its guard.

The British, with foreknowledge of an imminent rising and of the landing of arms from Germany, saw it as logical that without arms the Volunteers had

abandoned plans for insurrection. Until now, despite
[54] advice to the contrary, notably from General Friend, GOC Irish Command, who would have had the Volunteers proclaimed an illegal organisation, the Chief Secretary, Augustine Birrell, and his Under Secretary, Sir Matthew Nathan, had thought it wise to allow Volunteer activity as a kind of safety valve. Prompted by the Viceroy, Lord Wimborne, Nathan cabled Birrell in London on Sunday for permission to make a large number of arrests. The Castle authorities thought they had time in hand, but they were wrong. At a meeting of the Military Council on the Sunday morning it was agreed that the rising would commence on Easter Monday. Instructions to report for duty were filtered down through the ranks of the Dublin Volunteers, many of whose officers were members of the IRB. Very many probably had no idea of what reporting for duty on this occasion was to entail. Even IRB members had no idea of what the men at the top were planning. General Mulcahy has noted that even on the eve of the rising many were just waiting for the Home Rule situation 'to develop naturally'.[2]

Dublin was in holiday mood as the Volunteers mustered on the morning of 24 April, Easter Monday. The suspicions of Military Intelligence had been lulled; the Castle was somnolent; Mac Néill believed that there was no longer any danger of an insurrection. Arthur Griffith was looking after his children, Mrs Griffith having gone to stay with her sister in Cork for two or three days. He realised that the Castle would almost certainly make arrests within the next few days and that inevitably he would be among the victims.

The first shots of the Rising were fired by men of Connolly's Citizen Army at noon. A police guard at the Castle, an Irishman, was killed and the guardroom was seized. The Castle could easily have been taken but no one dreamed that it was sparsely defended. Liam O'Briain took the news to Mac Néill, who could scarcely believe it but resolved that his place was with the Volunteers. As so often before, he changed his mind. O'Briain himself returned to the city to look for his Volunteer company but joined the Citizen Army contingent under Michael Mallin and Countess Markiewicz which had occupied St Stephen's Green.

Connolly, Pearse and Plunkett led a column of about 150 Volunteers and Citizen Army men, variously armed and accoutred, to the General Post Office (GPO), which they seized and barricaded. A crowd gathered, and from the steps of the GPO Patrick Pearse read the historic Proclamation of the Republic, signed 'on behalf of the Provisional Government' by Thomas J. Clarke, Sean Mac Diarmada, P. H. Pearse, James Connolly, Thomas MacDonagh, Eamonn Ceannt and Joseph Plunkett, all of whom knew that they had probably signed their own death warrants. 'Thanks be to God, Pearse, that we have lived to see this day,' exclaimed Connolly, but Pearse's ringing words touched few hearts in the crowd. Hostility, curiosity, indifference, astonishment predominated. Many people were too stunned to react at all.

Other buildings were taken over, the South Union building by Ceannt and Cathal Brugha, the Four Courts by Edward Daly, the Mendicity Institute by Sean Heuston. The still unknown Eamon de Valera occupied Boland's Mill; Thomas MacDonagh moved his men, among them John MacBride, into Jacob's biscuit factory. Mallin was at Stephen's Green and there were a number of outposts. In all, about 700 men were involved, who were to be reinforced by a few hundred more as Volunteers who had not received instructions heard of the action and hastened to help.

Arthur Griffith heard the news as he set out from

home to take the children to their grandmother's. Instead, he left them with a neighbour and, Colum tells us, proceeded to the GPO to offer his services. There he talked to Sean MacDermott (or Mac Diarmada as he had signed the Proclamation). A statement made by Michael Noyk, the young Jewish lawyer whom Griffith had first met in 1910, and whose services were to be much appreciated by Michael Collins, suggests that Griffith had not gone in person to the GPO.[3]

Liam O'Briain informed Noyk that Griffith had told him he had sent a message 'telling them what he thought of them for leaving him in the dark' but volunteering to join them. The answer he got was that 'they wanted his pen and his brain to survive the fight for their memory – and not to join in'. Griffith saw the Rising as a wonderful but futile gesture. He was convinced that the Volunteers would be needed if the British government were to introduce conscription in Ireland and he would rather they had not been wasted. But the die was cast and he could only wish for success. He and Mac Néill discussed the possibility of an appeal to the whole country to rise, to take the pressure off Dublin, but it was not practicable. Neither attempted to go into hiding. When the end came, as it must, they would stand with the Volunteers.

The British took no serious action until Tuesday but methodically established their own posts, piercing the Volunteer cordon. There could be no doubt about the outcome but as the garrisons held out as day followed day, some of the hostility of the populace dissolved in admiration, even pride.

Incendiary shells set the heart of Dublin on fire. More shells from the gunboat *Helga* in the Liffey reduced buildings to rubble. The British, now commanded by Major-General Sir John Maxwell, were relentless. On Saturday, with the brave Elizabeth O'Farrell acting as go-between, Pearse endeavoured to negotiate terms but in the end was forced to surrender unconditionally. Miss O'Farrell had the sad duty of carrying the news to the other strongholds. To the jeers of the crowd the rebels marched into captivity. Rebels had 'come out' elsewhere too. Using guerrilla tactics, Thomas Ashe and Richard Mulcahy had overwhelmed a detachment of the Royal Irish Constabulary at Ashbourne and agreed to surrender only after Mulcahy had been taken by the British to see Pearse. From Enniscorthy Captains Etchingham and Doyle were also taken to Pearse before they were persuaded to capitulate. In Galway, Volunteers under Liam Mellows were forced to surrender. Confusion created by Mac Néill and news of the *Aud*'s sinking had frustrated the plans of the Cork Volunteers but, a few days later, the four Kent brothers fought with soldiers and police until their ammunition was exhausted. Thomas Kent was hanged a week later.

Stranded in Cork, Mrs Griffith made contact with the Volunteer leaders, Terence MacSwiney and Tomás MacCurtain, both of whom by their deaths were later to make a significant contribution to Irish independence. Mrs Griffith was unable to return to Dublin for another week during which no news of her husband and children reached her. When at last she arrived home, it was to her immense relief that she found them all safe. But Griffith knew very well that he would not have his freedom for long. As the British military authorities and the RIC began to round up known dissidents, it was inconceivable that the acknowledged founder and leader of Sinn Féin, whose every move had been watched for years, would be overlooked. Suddenly the name Sinn Féin had become attached to the Volunteers. They were Sinn Féiners; the rising was called a Sinn Féin rebellion. And yet the majority had never belonged to Griffith's organisation and many took umbrage at the misnomer.

When he was arrested, Griffith may have been apprehensive about his ultimate fate, but he must have known, also, that if he had not been arrested, his political stature would have been much reduced and his political future probably non-existent. He was taken to Richmond Barracks. It was 3 May, the day that Pearse, Clarke and MacDonagh were executed by firing squad at Kilmainham. Griffith's reaction to the news, Colum tells us, was a longing for 'vengeance on the murderers'.

Maxwell had been given plenary powers to deal with the situation. General courts martial were set up almost from the moment of surrender. Ninety death sentences were passed but seventy-five of these were commuted to life imprisonment. Even in this tenebrous atmosphere, Maxwell baulked at sending a woman, Countess Markiewicz, to the firing squad and Eamon de Valera escaped, probably because of his American origin, perhaps because even Maxwell decided that retribution had gone far enough.

Most of the leaders of the rising were not just nationalist zealots but writers and poets. Their nationalism and their poetry were inseparable and so they left to posterity not only the record of their deeds of sacrifice but moving testaments. Their courts martial addresses, their last words uttered and written, have been woven into the fabric of Irish history. Sir John Maxwell demanded altogether fifteen lives, including that of Thomas Kent in Cork. The executions were dragged out over nine suspense-laden days, and even after MacDermott and the grievously wounded Connolly were shot on 12 May, the suspense endured for several days before it was apparent that the last of the terse announcements of sentences carried out had been posted. There was to be one more; Sir Roger Casement was tried at the Old Bailey for treason and hanged on 3 August.

In the harsh climate of the First World War, when about three hundred shell-shocked young British soldiers were put to death for what was called cowardice, it was understandable that a British government should take strong punitive measures against men who had traded with the enemy and mounted an insurrection which had cost 450 lives, but they must have known that every Irish rebel executed had ever after lived in song and verse and in the hearts of the Irish people. It was true that the rebels had little sympathy from their compatriots, that their own press denounced them, that the leaders of the Irish Parliamentary Party called for punishment 'swift and stern', but a degree of magnanimity would have been wise.

There were too many executions and in some cases there was little justification for them. Old South African scores against John MacBride were settled, William Pearse was shot because he was a leader's brother, others – Edward Daly, Michael Mallin, Sean Heuston, for example – because their valour had marked them out. Throughout, Maxwell showed no grain of humanity. As each grim day passed, attitudes changed. Redmond, Dillon, even Carson urged clemency. The British cabinet was uneasy. As early as 6 May, with Maxwell present, it agreed 'to leave to his discretion the dealing with particular cases, subject to a general instruction that death should not be inflicted except upon ringleaders and proved murderers, and that it is desirable to bring the executions to a close as soon as possible'[4]. Maxwell could not be said to have followed the spirit of that general instruction and a stronger cabinet would have left less to his discretion.

5
The New Sinn Féin

Sean T. O'Kelly arrived at Reading jail in July to find about thirty internees already there, Griffith among them. He looked smaller than ever, O'Kelly thought, perhaps because he wore old carpet slippers tied with string instead of 'the queer shaped boots with high heels made for him by Barry's of Capel Street.'[1] Many thought that Griffith wore the high heels from vanity; in fact, he had been born with slightly deformed feet and needed the support of the heels. Even with them he was inclined to waddle and it was this mannerism which had amused a South African native who called him *Cuguan*, the Kaffir word for dove, which Griffith adopted as one of his many pseudonyms.

Griffith had also grown a beard, reported first by Michael Noyk who saw him in Wandsworth prison before his transfer to Reading.[2] In a letter to Lil Williams from Reading Griffith also alluded, rather proudly, to his beard, which he said 'shocked even the Military Guard – one of whom, known to us as The Looter, told me it was appalling even to his cold eye and twice appealed to me to let him shave it off.'[3]

It seemed that in prison Griffith relaxed as he never was able to relax with the self-imposed burden of Ireland's future on his shoulders. 'He behaved like the leading spirit in a party of holiday makers more or less isolated on a ship during a long voyage'[4] Ernest Blythe told Colum. His letters, most of which were smuggled out, were light-hearted; he organised chess tournaments, played handball with zest and attended Irish classes. About one-quarter of the internees were fluent Irish speakers. All the Irish provinces were represented and, wrote Griffith, 'all the Irish religious creeds – Catholic, Protestant and Dissenter.'[5] Referring to the classes he told Flo Williams that they were thinking of applying for affiliation to the Gaelic League.[6]

Griffith's wonderful fund of Irish songs helped keep up the morale of his fellows and he also produced a weekly manuscript journal with an admixture of humorous tales and verse and serious political writing.

When his wife visited Griffith in prison, the governor, Captain Morgan, who had warmed to the lively crowd of Irish internees, arranged for them to have some time together alone. They did not know then how soon they were to be reunited. Writing to Lily Williams, Griffith said that, unlike Frongoch, things at Reading moved smoothly as a rule, the governor being a Welshman and a gentleman.[7]

With the Irish internees were German prisoners of war and Griffith wrote that the main amusement of them all was to listen for the Zeppelin alarm. They were safe from bombing, he declared, perhaps with tongue in cheek, because Huntley and Palmer, the famous bakers, were next door to the jail. Huntley and Palmer were generous subscribers to government funds and it was to safeguard them from Zeppelin bombs that German and Irish prisoners were kept at Reading, Griffith claimed. 'Business is business,' he commented caustically.

In the same long letter to Lily Williams he said the internees knew only in a general way what was happening in Ireland, adding that his 'well-meaning but feather-headed friend Herbert Pim seems to be muddling up Sinn Féin a bit'. Griffith's guess was that Lloyd George, Carson and Redmond were planning to kick out Balfour and Asquith. They would then pass

a bogus Home Rule Bill and try to get the Irish to
[62] accept conscription. In that case 'Ireland must fight
conscription with tongues, pens, sticks, stones, pitchforks, swords, guns and all the other resources of civilisation.'

Griffith was hardly fair to Redmond for, when conscription in Ireland was mooted by the British government, Redmond fought it bitterly. He also battled for the freedom of the Irishmen interned after the Easter Rising. But Griffith was right in predicting Asquith's political demise and Lloyd George's accession to the head of the cabinet table. But Lloyd George was either more generous or wiser than Griffith had allowed and lost no time in releasing the last six hundred or so of the thousand men interned after the rising. The lesser lights had been released, batch by batch, over a period of several months.

The men at Reading had already decorated a Christmas tree when news of their release reached them. Happily they bequeathed the tree to the German prisoners and returned home. On Christmas Eve Arthur Griffith was reunited with his wife and children.

As for the 'bogus Home Rule Bill', it did not eventuate. Earlier, Asquith had made an attempt to dust down the 1914 Act shelved at the outbreak of war together with the Amending Bill, never debated, which provided for either four or six of the Ulster counties to be excluded. After the rising Asquith spent six days in Dublin, arriving on 12 May, the day of the last two executions – of Connolly and MacDermott. He talked to prisoners, read the court-martial speeches of the dead leaders and began to perceive the reasons for the rising. In attempting to revive the Home Rule issue he was trying to put together the broken pieces of Ireland as much as he was seeking to placate America. Again Ulster proved the sticking point; the cabinet decided that 'Sir E. Carson's claim for the definitive exclusion of Ulster could not be resisted'.[8] Redmond, who had been persuaded by Lloyd George that partition would be a temporary expedient, withdrew his support when he learned that Carson had been assured of its permanence. America gave the British government an affable nod in recognition of the attempt and Griffith wrote joyously from Reading jail: 'We buried the Partition Bill the other night with all solemnities.'[9]

Back in Dublin, Arthur Griffith, now forty-five, recognised that the rising had produced a totally new climate, that the Hungarian parallel now seemed a remote concept to a people who had witnessed violence and destruction in their own city, but he did not relinquish his conviction that Ireland's way to equality with Britain was to withdraw from the Westminster parliament and to establish her own parliament and organs of government. His own reputation and that of Sinn Féin had been enhanced adventitiously by the widespread adoption of the name Sinn Féin for the Volunteer movement and Herbert Pim, who had seemed 'to be muddling up Sinn Féin a bit' had kept the name of Arthur Griffith prominently before the readers of *The Irishman* which he edited. Griffith now began to prepare for the resuscitation of *Nationality*.

Sinn Féin branches were again proliferating as the 'silent majority', moved to anger by the executions and beginning to be disillusioned with the Parliamentary Party, recalled Griffith's aims. Arthur Griffith had been prepared to wait patiently for many years until people accepted his teaching. He had long believed that there would be no need for violence, that essentially his task was to educate public opinion. Ironically, it was because of the rising and its aftermath that people were ready to learn so much sooner than he had expected.

There was no sudden conversion to Sinn Féin and

many had little time either for Sinn Féin or its founder. [64] The physical force movement waxed strong, particularly among the young men from Frongoch, that university of revolution, many of whom resented the Sinn Féin label. Where there was common consent was in the desire of people, sickened by the ruthlessness of England's generals and the blindness of her politicians, to be free of England. Among them were many who at the outbreak of the rising had seen it as indefensible.

In February 1917 came the first indication of the turn of the political tide when Count Plunkett, father of the executed Joseph Mary Plunkett, contested a by-election at Roscommon as an independent and won by a large majority. He had the support of disparate elements of the nationalist movement, including Griffith and the fiery Michael Collins who, at this time, could be said to represent only the physical force element. Count Plunkett declined to take his seat at Westminster, a decision dictated by his own conscience rather than the persuasiveness of Arthur Griffith. Plunkett, indeed, advocated an entirely new national organisation, the first aim of which would be to put Ireland's case to the Peace Conference when finally the war came to an end. He convened an assembly at which Collins and Griffith met, probably for the first time. Plunkett's aim was popular but not new and did not lead to the fusion of the various groups.

Britain, sorely pressed, and long anxious for American participation in the war, was relieved when the United States declared war on 4 April 1917. Lloyd George was very conscious of the influence of Irish-Americans and anxious to rub ointment on Irish wounds; he was also apprehensive of the pervasive influence of Sinn Féin. When Joseph McGuinness, a prisoner in Lewes jail, won the Longford by-election early in May, he reacted very quickly, offering Redmond immediate Home Rule. But the same old Ulster snag was there; six counties would be excluded from its operation for five years, their ultimate future still to be decided. Redmond declined, knowing that the exclusion of part of their country would not be acceptable to the majority of Irish people.

As an alternative, Lloyd George suggested a convention which would bring together representatives of every interested body. Sinn Féin would be among them but outvoted, both Redmond and the Prime Minister hoped, by representatives from the Church, the unions and a host of others. In this way the spectre of a republic would be exorcised. To help create the right atmosphere, Lloyd George released the men of the rising who had been given prison sentences, among them some like Eamon de Valera and William Cosgrave whose death sentences had been commuted.

They returned as heroes and de Valera at once sent to the American President and Congress, in the name of the Provisional Government of the Republic of Ireland, a declaration of its intention to establish the right, which was the right of all small nations, to independence.

The first anniversary of the rising had passed quietly but the flag of the Republic had flown at half mast over the wrecked GPO on Easter Monday, a gentle reminder that the lives of men can be taken easily enough but their faith survives. For the moment, however, there was no certainty as to how that faith was to be sustained. For all the shades of opinion there were really two main strains of thought, that of the physical force men, with the reviving IRB in the vanguard, who were aiming at nothing less than a republic, and the Sinn Féin ideal, with Arthur Griffith still clinging to the conviction that a political framework on the model of 1782 was the only form of independent government which might allay the fears of the Unionist minority in Ulster. He offered a constructive policy hammered out in his mind and on countless pages over many years, a means of making an alternative government work. He knew that somehow the two elements, the guns and the strategy, had to come together and was no longer confident that the guns would not have to be used.

On July 10, Eamon de Valera easily won the parliamentary seat of East Clare at a by-election caused by the death on active service of Willie Redmond, brother of the leader of the Parliamentary Party. In August, William Cosgrave was elected for Kilkenny. The lanky de Valera was a raw politician, and a clumsy but sincere and effective speaker. He had that indefinable quality which stamps the leader. Arthur Griffith was impressed and perhaps saw in him something of the quality of William Rooney whom he had once thought would become Ireland's man of destiny. On 26 October, de Valera succeeded Arthur Griffith as President of Sinn Féin at the annual convention, or Ard Fheis, at the Mansion House in Dublin.

Well beforehand, Arthur Griffith, Cathal Brugha and de Valera had private meetings to work out a policy acceptable to both wings of the nationalist movement. Griffith saw no reason to amend the old Sinn Féin programme, Brugha wanted a proclamation of the Republic and no nonsense. It was de Valera who, only a week before the Ard Fheis, drafted the enigmatic formula which was first to unite and later to divide the parties: 'Sinn Féin aims at securing international recognition of Ireland as an independent Irish Republic. Having achieved that status the Irish people may by referendum freely choose their own form of Government.'

On the evening before the Ard Fheis Sean T. O'Kelly was summoned to Walter Cole's house in Mountjoy Square[10]. Cole was a friend of Griffith's. In Reading jail they had frequently read together an Irish version of the Gospels – with the English version beside them. Also at Cole's house were Henry Dixon, John O'Mahony and Arthur Griffith. Cole wanted to make sure that Griffith would stand for re-election as President of Sinn Féin. O'Mahony and Dixon were convinced he would lose to de Valera. Griffith was not militant enough for the Volunteers or the IRB. O'Kelly counselled Griffith to withdraw rather than suffer humiliation. Griffith listened in his impassive way but said nothing. Next day he withdrew and so did Count Plunkett who had also been nominated.

Arthur Griffith had never been personally ambitious. He had stepped diffidently into the shoes he himself had made for William Rooney. Now he stepped out of them and humbly put them at the feet of Eamon de Valera in whom, he said, 'we have a soldier and a statesman'. He regretted that drastic changes had been made to the constitution of Sinn Féin but he recognised that men younger than himself, who had already done battle with the British and acquitted themselves well, wanted action quickly. At least they had accepted his basic concept of an alternative Irish assembly. For the first time, the name Dáil Éireann was heard. When, the day after the Sinn Féin convention, de Valera was elected President of the Volunteers, the chain was complete. Michael Collins had been elected to the Sinn Féin executive, so bringing the IRB into the circle. Griffith himself became vice-president and his nominee, the colourful Darrell Figgis, was voted joint secretary with Austin Stack who was in prison.

Meanwhile, Lloyd George's monumental convention meandered on, achieving little but to allow him to keep face with America. Sinn Féin, the Volunteers, even the Irish Labour Party had ignored it. The majority wrote it off as a ploy to placate America and as a launching pad for conscription.

Henry Duke, Chief Secretary for Ireland, was con-
[68] vinced that failure of the convention would necessitate rule by force in Ireland and 'matters would drift into a state of affairs which could hardly be controlled'.[11] The cabinet were agreed that the only possible solution to the Irish problem was 'one Parliament for the whole of Ireland, sitting in Dublin'. True, it was proposed to retain control of police and customs but, had the cabinet stuck to it, they could have put forward a proposal which was at least negotiable and was certainly an improvement on the recently made offer which involved partition.

The growing demand for self-determination was alarming the British government, already preoccupied with the frightful and nationally debilitative war. As yet, the raw American troops had made no great impact and the drain on British manpower seemed unstemmable. Britain simply could not afford trouble on the doorstep. Men were jailed for making 'seditious' speeches or for parading or drilling in Volunteer uniform, misdemeanours which no longer seemed reprehensible to the general populace. By September of 1917 there were about thirty such prisoners in Mountjoy. Some, among them Austin Stack and Thomas Ashe, resorted to hunger strike. Ashe, who, with Mulcahy, had won the only victory of the rising, and who had recently been elected President of the Supreme Council of the reconstituted IRB, died from complications following forcible feeding. His funeral at Glasnevin, following a lying in state, took place on 30 September and attracted huge crowds who were deeply moved both by his death and by the grandeur of the occasion. Wisely the authorities refrained from arresting uniformed Volunteers.

In February 1918, the cabinet authorised Duke to proclaim Sinn Féin a dangerous association in some areas and to arrest and intern likely troublemakers.

Overnight, the Home Secretary thought of a snag. As the Sinn Féin leaders were British subjects (a status they were all too anxious to forgo), it would be necessary to prove legally hostile association, he explained to the cabinet.[12]

This hardly seemed the moment to extend conscription to Ireland but casualties on the Western Front were fearful and the cabinet were desperate. Even so they were hesitant. The measure proposed was primarily to enable the government to dredge up half a million men in Great Britain itself but it was calculated that a further 150,000 men could be raised in Ireland.

At the same time a Home Rule Bill, with Ulster excluded again, was offered. It could hardly have been more clumsily timed. Lloyd George saw it, or persuaded himself that he saw it, as the fulfilment of a pledge to Sir Horace Plunkett, chairman of the long-running convention, that a Home Rule Bill in line with the convention's report would be offered. Indeed, the Military Service Bill *in toto* was delayed to await that report. But the Prime Minister did not help matters when he blandly insisted that the young Irishmen compulsorily drafted for service under the Union Jack 'should feel that they are not fighting for establishing a principle abroad that is denied to them at home'.

There was not the remotest possibility that the agreement of the Irish to conscription could be bought. Henry Duke, who was a realist, remarked, 'We might almost as well conscript Germans.' The loss of Ireland would result, he prophesied.[13]

Long before the Military Service Bill was introduced in the House of Commons – on 10 April – and despite the secrecy with which it had been surrounded, the gist of it was common knowledge in Dublin. In the House the Irish Parliamentary Party, led by Dillon since Redmond's death in March, vigorously opposed [70] the bill and, in the end, stormed out. Two days later, on 18 April, Dillon and Devlin appeared on the same platform as de Valera and Griffith, at an anti-conscription protest meeting organised by the Lord Mayor, Laurence O'Neill, at the Mansion House in Dublin. At that meeting almost every skein of Irish opinion came together.

In Sinn Féin ranks there had been some doubt about appearing on the same platform as members of the Parliamentary Party. Griffith insisted that the people wanted them to do so and, in Colum's view, 'probably saved Sinn Féin as a popular force by taking that line'.[14]

Henry Duke had warned the cabinet that the Nationalist MPs would probably abandon Westminster and 'make common cause with the Sinn Féiners'.[15] Their attendance at the Mansion House conference following their walkout at Westminster was tantamount to an admission that Sinn Féin had been right all along. At the conference the Sinn Féin delegates took the lead. The veteran, William O'Brien, was impressed by Griffith's 'placid strength and assuredness', and noted de Valera's 'transparent sincerity' and 'the obstinacy with which he would defend a thesis, as though it were a point in pure mathematics'.[16]

It was de Valera who composed the declaration which was unanimously passed by the conference. Taking their stand on Ireland's 'separate and distinct nationhood', the delegates denied 'the right of the British Government or any external authority to impose compulsory military service in Ireland against the clearly expressed wish of the Irish people'. The passing of the Conscription Bill was 'regarded as a declaration of war on the Irish nation.' The declaration concluded, 'The attempt to enforce it will be an unwarrantable aggression, which we call upon all Irishmen to resist by the most effective means at their disposal.' A pledge on the same lines but in simpler form, it was suggested, 'should be solemnly taken in every parish in the country on the following Sunday'.

The outcome of all this was a swing to Sinn Féin among Nationalist Party supporters. A by-election was pending in the Ulster county of Cavan and Sinn Féin put forward Arthur Griffith as their candidate. The Volunteers were out in strength to support him. Meanwhile, the British government were giving much time to working out how to enforce conscription. It was recognised that the 15,000 troops already stationed in Ireland would have to be reinforced and Lord French was dispatched to Dublin to work out a plan of action. Lloyd George was also anxious to pass a Home Rule Bill as quickly as possible, though it meant putting his government at risk. The nature of stick and carrot decided upon, the next essential was to remove the men who were likely to persuade the people not to be coerced by the one or tempted by the other.

The Home Secretary, Sir George Cave, suggested amending Section 14B of the Defence of the Realm Regulations so that the Sinn Féin leaders could be interned without proof of hostile association.[17] There were rumours that de Valera had been in contact with the Germans but even the cabinet conceded there was nothing in them, nor did they know of any *Aud* or Casement this time.

Impressed by French's report of the situation, the government appointed him Lord Lieutenant. Edward Shortt replaced Duke as Chief Secretary. French told the cabinet that he intended to put a stop to German intrigues. He took up his appointment on 11 May. On 17 May, he issued a proclamation alleging the involvement of Sinn Féin in what became known as the 'German Plot' and over seventy arrests were made that night.

To the Irish the episode was a blatant 'frame-up' to get the Sinn Féin activists out of the way, and certainly that was the desired outcome. The evidence when produced was flimsy and implicated the American-Irish rather than Sinn Féin. Only the landing from a German submarine of a former Connaught Ranger named Dowling, who had been suborned by Casement, lent the allegations a touch of authenticity. For the rest, rumours and hearsay, odd incidents which could be given a sinister interpretation and perhaps a touch of the spy hysteria which gripped Great Britain during the war together made a case which some at least of Lloyd George's ministers persuaded themselves was genuine.

Through Michael Collins, whose intelligence system was steadily being built up, members of the Sinn Féin executive and others were warned of the exact hour of their arrests. It was decided there was more political profit to be gained from allowing them to take place. The British government had blundered again but they were men under almost unimaginable pressure and inevitably made obvious moves without thinking them through to their likely consequences. De Valera, Griffith, and Griffith's old friend Maud Gonne were among more than seventy men and women who were packed off to English prisons. Collins himself, Cathal Brugha, Richard Mulcahy and others who were needed to organise the Volunteers for the armed conflict which now seemed inevitable evaded capture.

From Gloucester prison Griffith wrote to Lil Williams on 19 June that he could see the tower of the cathedral from his cell. As it seemed to be 'a piece of architecture worth admiring', he assumed, though he knew nothing of Gloucester's history, 'that it was built not by the English but by their Norman French Conquerers.'[18] This may have been another example of Griffith's refusal to recognise good in anything English, but one suspects that there might have been disgruntled humour in the remark for he reminded Robert Brennan that 'he did not exactly despise Shakespeare and Shelley', when Brennan expressed surprise that Griffith had admired the cathedral.[19]

In Gloucester, as in Reading jail in 1916, Griffith made the most of his captivity. No doubt it helped when he heard that he had won the Cavan by-election. A prolific letter writer, he had ample time for his correspondence, most of which went by surreptitious means from the prison.

Official channels apparently were less reliable. Writing to Thomas Martin in London on 16 July,[20] he complained that an earlier letter had been returned to him, the British government having refused to transmit it. He said this was happening frequently. 'The annoyance caused to us by this malicious proceeding is borne with equanimity,' he told Martin. To people he knew well, like the Williams sisters, he wrote in hasty scribble, but he was considerate of those who were not familiar with his handwriting and took care that it was legible.

In a letter dated 17 October[21] to Seamus O'Sullivan (addressed in his real name of James Starkey), Griffith mentioned that Desmond Fitzgerald had become an excellent handball player, while McEntee, he wrote, 'frequently fires off a sonnet'. His reason for writing to O'Sullivan was to send condolences on the death of his father. It was characteristic of Griffith that even in prison he was both thoughtful and punctilious. He mentioned that Denis MacCullough and Dr Dillon had shaken off mild attacks of influenza. Later, the notorious influenza epidemic which made deep inroads into European populations was to strike in the prison. Griffith, it seems, caught the disease but fought it off by taking a whole bottle of quinine.[22] But two Irish prisoners died.

In the absence of the political leaders in English [74] prisons Michael Collins quickly became the dominant figure in the Irish scene. Within the compass of six years Collins, an almost unknown young Volunteer officer in the Easter Rising, became one of the nation's leaders. He was the complete revolutionary, a powerful, tempestuous, engaging man, able to turn his mind to almost any problem. And he did, often treading on the toes of others who saw the problem as theirs.

The British cabinet continued to wrangle about conscription, decided to try to raise volunteers instead (not without some success), discussed Home Rule and a federation of England, Scotland, Wales and Ireland, and condemned the intervention of the Catholic hierarchy on the conscription issue. Finally, as the German armies began to collapse, the whole Irish Question was shelved. It little mattered now; the damage had been done; the Irish were almost completely alienated. In Ireland itself, Lord French did his best to eliminate all nationalist organisations. Relying on the Defence of the Realm Act, he declared Sinn Féin, the Volunteers, Cumann na mBan, even the Gaelic League, dangerous organisations. Assemblies and processions in public places were prohibited — but flourished just the same. Men were arrested for making speeches and for singing Irish songs. There were raids on private houses, arrests, trials and sentences. But the orators continued to make speeches, the people to sing their songs, and the Volunteers daily increased their strength and quietly went on training and drilling. Michael Collins, Adjutant-General and Director of Organisation; Cathal Brugha, Chief of Staff; and the little-known Richard Mulcahy, Deputy Chief of Staff, with much talented assistance, re-organised the Volunteers. Collins worked secretly, too, extending his intelligence network and revitalising the IRB of whose Supreme Council he was now a member. Sinn Féin, now accommodating people of many shades of opinion, had become rambling and amorphous. Harry Boland, Collins's great friend and IRB colleague, set to work to streamline the organisation. Sinn Féin became much more militant.

In December 1918, almost before the clamour of churchbells proclaiming the armistice had died away, a general election was called. In Britain, 'Hang the Kaiser' was the catch-cry. Ireland was almost forgotten – until the election results were known. Despite some hostility, especially from Irish soldiers – Sinn Féin headquarters in Harcourt Street were wrecked – despite censorship of the Sinn Féin manifesto and despite the enforced absence from the hustings of forty-eight of their candidates, the party won seventy-three of 105 seats in the thirty-two counties. The old Parliamentary Party won six. Sinn Féin had simply taken over from the Parliamentary Party as the dominant party of the people, who had voted for them in the knowledge that not one Sinn Féin member would take his seat at Westminster.

Although Sinn Féin did not have an overall majority of votes over the whole country – in other words, more people voted against a republic – the Sinn Féin and Nationalist votes combined completely overwhelmed support for the Unionists.

6
Fight for Freedom

It was galling for Griffith to be locked up in Gloucester jail when the party he had created, if not altogether recognisable as such, ultimately triumphed; galling too for its leader, Eamon de Valera, in the fastness of Lincoln jail. To him Griffith gave total allegiance. 'I have complete confidence in de Valera,' he said, ending a discussion among prisoners in Gloucester.[1]

The National Assembly envisaged by Griffith now came into being, conveniently elected under the British electoral system. There was confidence now that with the backing of the Peace Conference, perhaps the one plank in Sinn Féin's platform which everyone understood and favoured, the new Assembly could treat on equal terms with the British parliament. President Wilson's famous Fourteen Points, which included the right of small nations to govern themselves, would provide the magic passport to 'international recognition of Ireland as an independent Irish republic'. Once that had been achieved, there remained the second tenet of the awkward formula to be tested, that 'the Irish people may by referendum freely choose their own form of Government'.

On 21 January 1919, at the Mansion House in Dublin, Dáil Éireann met for the first time, though there had been preliminary meetings on the 7th and 14th. It was a sadly depleted Assembly. Of the sixty-nine elected Sinn Féin candidates, four of whom, including Griffith, represented two constituencies, only twenty-seven were present. Most of the rest were still in prison; Collins and Boland were in Lincoln sizing up the chances of releasing de Valera. With their help, de Valera, Sean Milroy and Sean McGarry broke jail on 3 February. Collins had organised their escape route and a few hours later they arrived safely in Manchester. The twenty-six Unionists and six Nationalists, though eligible for the Dáil, chose to take their seats at Westminster.

In de Valera's absence, Cathal Brugha was elected temporary President of the Dáil. A provisional constitution was approved and a Declaration of Independence read. This ratified the establishment of the Irish republic proclaimed by Pearse from the GPO portico on Easter Monday of 1916. All hopes were focussed on the Peace Conference, which had opened the previous day and to which the Dáil named its delegates — de Valera, Griffith and Count Plunkett.

The British government did not intend to allow the Dáil to usurp its powers in Ireland and knew they would have to reckon with physical force. Lloyd George was determined that the onus of shooting first should be on the 'rebels'. On the day that Dáil Éireann met for the first time the rebels did shoot first. At Soloheadbeg members of the South Tipperary Brigade ambushed and shot dead two RIC men who were escorting a cart carrying gelignite to a quarry. The late Dan Breen, who took part in the ambush, told me that the intention was 'to light the fuse'. Deliberate or not, the action, which had little to commend it, certainly did that.

The Tipperary men went on the run but one of them, seventeen-year-old Sean Hogan, was taken by police on 12 May. His comrades audaciously rescued him from a train at Knocklong. In the fray a sergeant and a constable were killed and the changing temper of the people was demonstrated by the inquest jury,

who refused to bring in a verdict of murder and in-
[78] stead blamed the government 'for exposing the police to danger'. They also took the opportunity to demand self-determination for Ireland. The change of heart occurred, not only because of people's admiration for the exploits of the hunted men and because a seventeen-year-old Irish boy had narrowly escaped a British rope, but because South Tipperary had been declared a military area with consequent restrictions on people's lives and the indignity of searches of homes, handbags and pockets. Anger and frustration were turned against the authorities.

On 4 February, Lord French sent the British cabinet three telegrams urging the immediate release of the 'German Plot' prisoners held in English prisons. The cabinet had been debating the question for some weeks and French had sternly opposed release. His sudden change perplexed the cabinet, who continued to argue until 4 March when at last they decided to release the prisoners gradually. De Valera could now safely reappear in Ireland. He had already been smuggled back to Dublin and had decided to undertake a mission to the United States. He was in Liverpool awaiting a ship when Arthur Griffith and the other internees were released.

The visit to America was postponed. Instead, de Valera would return to Ireland. A great ceremony of welcome at Mount Street Bridge, where men under his command had fought magnificently during the rising, was planned. He was to receive the freedom of the city of Dublin. On instructions from London, any such ceremony or procession was proclaimed by the Castle administration.

Arthur Griffith, who had returned almost unnoticed, presided at a meeting of the Sinn Féin executive when the British proclamation was discussed. In *Recollections of the Irish War* Darrell Figgis makes clear what happened. Figgis questioned whether the executive had ever sanctioned the ceremony. Collins left them in no doubt that the decision had been taken by 'the proper body, the Irish Volunteers'. Vehemently he asserted that 'the sooner fighting was forced and a general state of disorder created through the country, the better it would be for the country'. Contemptuously he told the executive that they had been called 'only to confirm what the proper people had decided'. Collins was saying that the physical force movement was now in charge, but Griffith put him down firmly. Not the Volunteer executive but the Sinn Féin executive would make the decision. It was decided that Griffith should consult de Valera, who agreed that defiance at the risk of civilian lives was not justified and returned quietly to Ireland.

Griffith had to accept that the Volunteers would be involved in the coming fight for freedom, but he was adamant that they should be subject to the Dáil. The difficulty was that so many Volunteers, who were responsible to their own executive, were also members of the Dáil. More insidiously, a number of them were members of what had again become a powerful secret organisation, the IRB.

What the Irish electorate now understood was anyone's guess. They had voted for self-determination but no mention had been made in the Sinn Féin manifesto that it was proposed to win it by force. On the other hand, they had elected men like Brugha, Collins, Mulcahy and de Valera himself, who had already demonstrated their belief in physical force. It could be claimed that there was at least tacit consent to the use of violence.

On 1 April, Eamon de Valera was elected President of the Dáil and the following day announced his chosen heads of department. Cathal Brugha was given the Department of Defence; Collins, Finance; Count

Plunkett, Foreign Affairs; Countess Markiewicz had responsibility for Labour; W. T. Cosgrave headed Local Government; and Arthur Griffith, soon to be Acting President, was made responsible for Home Affairs. Richard Mulcahy was appointed Chief of Staff by the Volunteer Executive of which de Valera was nominally head, and later became Assistant Minister for Defence. Other portfolios were allotted to Eoin Mac Néill (Industries), Robert Barton (Agriculture) and Lawrence Ginnell (Propaganda).

Much of the Dáil business in those early April sessions concerned international recognition of the Irish Republic, but one cruelly effective measure on the home front was passed. This, the ostracism of members of the RIC, was de Valera's own brainchild. 'They must be shown and made to feel how base are the functions they perform, and how vile is the position they occupy,' he pronounced.

The RIC was a quasi-military organisation and at the best of times Ireland was heavily policed. Even quite modest towns boasted a police barracks accommodating what amounted to a small garrison. Dublin Castle relied heavily on RIC reports from all over the country, for the policemen knew their own areas and their own communities well and generally served them well. Many were family men, well liked and respected, but there was no denying that they were an essential part of the Castle's intelligence system and as such inimical to the Volunteers. Throughout the War of Independence, which was now gathering momentum, the RIC, standing as they believed for law and order, were prime adversaries of the IRA. Some resigned, to be replaced later on by the egregious Black and Tans, designated by the British government as a special police force, government policy being to treat the activities of the IRA as criminal violence and not military action. Other RIC men threw in their lot with the IRA. The majority stuck to their posts, hoped to avoid trouble but faced it with courage when it came.

Early in its life the Dáil had discussed a social policy which owed much to Griffith's long publicised ideas and not a little to James Connolly. Not much could be done but the various departments attempted to set up some kind of administrative machinery. But first the Dáil coffers required to be filled and Collins's organising genius was to prove equal to the task.

Britain frustrated Ireland's attempt to be heard at the Peace Conference, holding that it was a domestic issue. Patrick McCartan in the United States and Sean T. O'Kelly in Paris, both described as ambassadors, succeeded in whipping up a good deal of support. In America the House of Representatives came out in favour of Ireland's sovereignty and an American Commission for Irish Freedom tried to intercede in Paris. Woodrow Wilson came under pressure but had no intention of breaking with Britain on the issue though, in fact, he had a strong weapon, had he wished to use it. Britain was desperately anxious that the Americans write down her enormous war debt.

De Valera had to admit defeat, though he, Griffith and Count Plunkett sent a memorandum, dated 26 May, to Clemenceau, President of the Peace Conference, to ensure that Ireland's case at least was on record. Meanwhile, the American Commission, unsuccessful in Paris, toured Ireland and addressed the Dáil. Their visit, implying large scale American support, boosted the morale of the Irish people. At the end of the war, Ireland had been offered no crumb of independence. It was plain that British governments offered Home Rule only when Irish votes were needed to help them stay in power, or when they resorted to bribery in order to push through a measure as unpopular as conscription or, finally, when physical force was used against them as at Easter 1916.

It was a lesson the Irish moderates were gradually
[82] absorbing. It was an eye-opener, too, when thousands of young Irishmen returned from the Western Front and, disillusioned, enlisted in the IRA. Among them were not only wartime soldiers but regular British army officers. Michael Collins was determined upon military action and again and again berated the Sinn Féin executive for their caution. Griffith had brought out a third edition of 'The Resurrection of Hungary' the previous year. He acknowledged that the Hungarian analogy was dated but firmly believed the ideas it contained were still germane. Now, in 1919, the Irish Assembly he had advocated for so long was in being, the administrative machinery, first to duplicate, and then supplant, the Castle's functions was being set up. He was still convinced that if all the people were to support the Dáil and its machinery of government, availing themselves of its courts and ignoring the established judicial system, paying taxes to the Dáil and withholding them from the British tax-collector, electing local councils which would have no commerce with Dublin Castle; if they were to offer passive resistance all along the line and accept the suffering which doubtless would be inflicted upon them, then Ireland could win her independence without resort to arms. But the tide was running strong now and Griffith had to allow himself to be carried with it or stand aside altogether. This man who did not relish violence but who had always recognised that armed force might be the only solution was for eighteen long months to preside over a government committed to a campaign of violence and destruction.

From June 1919 until December 1920, Griffith's chief was absent in America. For de Valera, too, clung to the hope that a non-violent solution was possible. He saw it still in terms of international recognition of Ireland as a sovereign state. De Valera believed that if he could mobilise public opinion in America, there might still be a way of putting pressure on Great Britain. In Paris a League of Nations was evolving; with powerful America on Ireland's side, the League itself might intercede. It was important to ensure, as he explained to the United States Congress in 1964, that in signing the League Covenant the United States 'was not pledging itself to maintain Ireland as an integral part of British territory.'[2] De Valera also knew that as President of the Dáil which, in American minds, was the same as President of Ireland, he was the man who could best promote the Irish National Loan.

With hindsight, it can be argued that his presence in Ireland would have been even more valuable, and many of his colleagues were surprised that he should wish to be anywhere else. He was not to be moved and there was eventually unanimous agreement in the cabinet, which Griffith made clear to the Dáil. De Valera could not be in two places at once and, while there simply was no one else who could have accomplished the American mission, the team he left in Ireland proved that they could manage without him. The one man who really was indispensable in the next two years was Michael Collins, who dominated the whole revolutionary movement.

By May, the Dáil was having to meet secretly, though it was not formally proscribed until September. Most of the members were soon wanted men and meetings became infrequent. A very mobile executive carried on its work, ministers having to move, complete with papers, from house to house, office to office to avoid capture. It is astonishing that the Sinn Féin government made any headway at all, particularly since most Dáil members were young men and few had experience even in local government.

With his customary flair, Collins arranged de Valera's secret voyage to America, where he arrived as a stow-

away on 11 June. Before his departure he nominated
[84] Arthur Griffith as Deputy President in his absence, and recommended that he be paid the presidential salary. Griffith was now forty-eight. He did not have the charisma of de Valera or Collins, nor was he a leader from choice; but in his reserved way he did have authority, which was buttressed by experience and by his long involvement in the nationalist cause.

Griffith was well aware that the Volunteers and the IRB were not going to be stopped by politicians. He turned his attention to the social programme announced when first Dáil Éireann met, a high-minded ideal which probably no government could ever hope to achieve but which did seek, by economic and social reforms, to create a fairer society, with the people of Ireland owning their country's resources. On 19 June 1919, Griffith moved in the Dáil that 'a Select Commission be appointed to inquire into the National Resources and present conditions of Manufacturing and Productive Industries in Ireland, and to consider and report by what means those Natural Resources may be fully developed, and how those industries may be encouraged and extended'.

It was a tall order, but Griffith saw that if the merger between the physical force and constitutional movements was to be preserved, the people and the members of the Dáil themselves should not lose sight of the fact that the Dáil had been elected on the Sinn Féin manifesto to form a government, not to run a clandestine army. Somehow he had to keep a balance. As it was, the relationship between the Dáil and the Volunteers was not very clearly defined. More nebulous still was the position of the IRB under whose constitution the President of the Supreme Council was President of the Republic of Ireland until a permanent republican government was established. It was at about this time that Michael Collins became President of the Supreme Council of the IRB.

De Valera had belonged uneasily to the IRB for a short time before the Easter Rising but did not rejoin. Cathal Brugha, once a fervent member, held that a secret organisation was now superfluous. Independence could be achieved in the open, he maintained. In his IRB capacity Collins commanded the loyalty of a large number of Volunteers in positions of responsibility. That he enjoyed this additional source of power created tensions, and Brugha was intensely suspicious. As Director of Intelligence on the Volunteers' General Headquarters Staff, Collins was subordinate to his Minister of Defence; in cabinet he was Brugha's equal. Brugha might have reconciled himself to this anomalous situation, but Collins's IRB activities were beyond his control, even his knowledge, and as they certainly impinged on the operations of the Volunteers, Brugha was resentful.

These tensions made Griffith's task of co-ordinating the functions of his ministers unenviable. He was exercised, too, by the dichotomy – which echoed the rift in the early days of Sinn Féin, when the young men of the Dungannon Clubs had taken a much more militant line than he – between the 'old' Sinn Féin and the physical force movement following their union in 1917. De Valera's formula had disguised it, but there were those in the cabinet for whom only the first part of the formula, the securing of international recognition of Ireland as an independent Irish Republic, counted; whereas Griffith was determined that once that had been achieved, the pledge that the Irish people should freely choose their own form of government should be honoured. Griffith revealed some of his apprehension in what amounted to a plea for unity when he addressed the Sinn Féin convention later in the year. He tried to identify Sinn Féin:

> Sinn Féin is not a party. It is a national composi-
[86] tion. If it is a party at all, it is a composite party. No part of that composition may claim its own individual programme until the national ideal of freedom has first been attained. Then we may press forward our separate ideals. Until then we must sink ourselves that the nation may gain from our unity.[3]

Griffith patently believed that once self-determination had been achieved, the two strands of Sinn Féin would separate, that two political parties would emerge to put their respective convictions to the people. Meanwhile, he exhorted the militants to concentrate on the achievement of freedom and leave Ireland's form of government to be settled when it was won, as he himself was prepared to do. Strangely, he not only accepted but advocated the Oath of Allegiance which was put to members and officers of Dáil Éireann in August, for the Oath contained the words: 'I will support and defend the Irish Republic and the Government of the Irish Republic which is Dáil Éireann, against all enemies, foreign and domestic, and I will bear true faith and allegiance to the same. . . .' For many this was an absolute commitment, allowing of no other form of government.

At their convention the Volunteers formally recognised their responsibility to the Minister for Defence and subsequently also took the Oath. So the Volunteers became a national army subject to political control, known officially as *Óglaigh na Éireann* and popularly as the Irish Republican Army, quickly shortened to IRA. Cathal Brugha, with de Valera's blessing, was mainly instrumental in bringing about the change, which must have been very welcome to Arthur Griffith for whom, paramount above all else, was that the Dáil, the elected body, should be, and hould be known to be, the responsible authority. f the Dáil were to disintegrate, all that would remain vould be an armed rebellion.

A Dáil Éireann National Loan was launched with target of £250,000. To ask the people to prove their upport and their confidence by reaching into their ockets was a real test. As Minister of Finance, the ncredible Collins found time to organise the bond-elling campaign and even sat at a table in the street ersonally signing bonds. The target figure was ex-eeded by over £100,000. In America, de Valera was minently successful in attracting loan funds. It was ot easy to 'salt away' such large sums, but it was nanaged.

The British government, confident at first that they ould contain this latest upsurge of nationalist fervour n Ireland, now became apprehensive. A clandestine overnment with its own army and ample funds was o charade. In the North, Carson was threatening o bring out the Ulster Volunteers if there were any ttempts to take away, in his lawyer's phrase, 'one jot r tittle' of the Protestant loyalists' rights as British itizens, which was of small comfort to Lloyd George, vho needed Unionist support to keep his hybrid overnment in power.

In Dublin, the Castle's intelligence service began to reak down as the Collins 'Squad', led by Patrick Daly, systematically began to pick off the detectives f G Division and as Collins's counter-intelligence ystem became ever more formidable. Among his gents were men in the Castle itself. Outside Dublin, RIC barracks were attacked and there were skirmishes n Tipperary, Limerick, Clare and elsewhere. Raids or arms were frequent, the most brilliant being the oarding of a British naval sloop in Bantry Bay. In December 1919 an abortive attempt on the life of the Lord Lieutenant, Lord French, was made. It was a

very near miss and Lloyd George and his cabinet nov
[88] realised the lengths to which the IRA were preparec to go. The British reacted in traditional style, combining coercion with concession.

On 22 December, the Better Government of Irelan Bill, soon to be known as the Partition Bill, was introduced in the House of Commons. It was not, as th Irish claimed, an attempt to 'divide and rule', bu simply the only compromise which seemed possible There were to be two parliaments, one for the twenty six counties of 'Southern Ireland', one for six countie in the irreconcilable North. The Unionists did no want their own parliament, preferring to remain a much a part of the British political system as Eas Anglia or London, but they began to see some advantages in it and Craig was able to persuade th government that the bill should apply to six counties not nine, so virtually ensuring the Unionists a permanent majority. A basis for future unity was offerec – a Council of Ireland to which both Northern an Southern parliaments were to nominate members The British government were to retain control o foreign affairs, defence, customs and excise and muc else. Once again, Britain had offered too little, to late, but the measure was not without potential an it is a pity that it was not offered as the basis for negotiated settlement. Two tragic years were to pas before it occurred to the British to sit round a tabl and talk of Ireland's future with her own representatives. As it was, the Irish people gave their verdict i local elections in January and June of 1920. Sin Féin became dominant in County Councils and Rura District Councils and controlled the majority of th Poor Law Boards.

In March 1920, the Black and Tans appeared, an even Lloyd George was to admit later that the Britis government had entered a 'dubious area'. Attache ɔ the RIC as temporary constables, the Black and 'ans were intended to restore 'law and order' quickly nd shock the Irish into accepting the 'better govern- ıent' prescribed for them. As far as possible, the ·ritish army kept out of the fighting, the government ıaintaining that what they persisted in describing as riminal violence and civil disobedience should be dealt ith by police action. Rather unwillingly, General Sir Ievil Macready became Commander-in-Chief of the ·ritish forces in Ireland. Sir Hamar Greenwood be- ame Chief Secretary.

The tempo of violence quickened. Killing and urning became commonplace. Reprisal followed eprisal. Collins was ruthless in eliminating dangerous dversaries. One was Alan Bell, who had been given he task of tracking down National Loan funds and ad begun to make inroads into them. Such killings ere seen on the Irish side as state executions, neces- arily carried out rather squalidly. The British had rison gallows and a professional hangman to call upon.

Tomás MacCurtain, Lord Mayor of Cork and Com- ıandant of Cork No. 1 Brigade IRA, was shot in is own home by Black and Tans. Plans he had made ɔr the formation of 'flying columns', small, mobile isciplined groups using guerrrilla tactics, were put into ffect by GHQ a few months later, and a new breed f Irish hero, the guerrilla leader, emerged – Tom arry, Sean MacEoin, Liam Lynch, Ernie O'Malley nd Michael Brennan, among others, became names ɔ conjure with.

The British banned all nationalist organisations. 'he jails were full and prisoners resorted to the hunger trike. In Brixton prison, Terence MacSwiney, Mac- Curtain's successor as Lord Mayor of Cork, fasted to eath. His seventy-four-day ordeal engendered sym- athy throughout the world and was a tremendous low for the Irish cause. So, too, was the execution

of Kevin Barry, an eighteen-year-old medical studen
[90] hanged on 1 November, the day of MacSwiney' funeral.

November 1920 was the blackest month of the wa On 21 November, 'Bloody Sunday', eleven British in telligence agents were shot dead in a carefully planne operation. That same afternoon, Black and Tans mas sacred fourteen people at a football match at Crok Park. The same day, two of Collins's men, Dick McKe and Peadar Clancy, with an innocent visitor, wer brutally tortured and killed. Later in the month, Ton Barry's flying column ambushed and killed eightee 'Auxiliaries', a force of mainly ex-officers which ha come into being as an adjunct to the Black and Tan in August.

On 10 December, French declared martial law i the south. Two days later, Black and Tans, infuriate by another successful ambush by Barry, poured int Cork and burned the heart of the city. The findin of a military inquiry into the incident was not pub lished because 'the effect of publishing the repor if Parliament was sitting would be disastrous to th Government's whole policy in Ireland.'[4]

A spate of arrests followed Bloody Sunday and on 26 November, Arthur Griffith, Eoin Mac Néil and Eamonn Duggan were imprisoned in Mountjoy Griffith had been expecting arrest for months. Hi home was raided continually, his small son had bee roughly interrogated. He seldom went home and neve stayed in one place for very long. It was his weddin anniversary which drew him home. Griffith's arres annoyed Lloyd George, who had already sounded hin out on proposals put forward by General Cockeril in a letter to *The Times*, but the Prime Minister di not order his release, probably deciding that he wa more easily accessible in Mountjoy.

In prison Griffith relaxed. 'Not only was he genial

but it was noted by some around him that he had an air as if things were going well.'[5] He could look back on the past months with a good deal of satisfaction. The Industrial Commission he had created had been analysing Ireland's resources and had accumulated much valuable data. Following Sinn Féin's success in the local elections, William Cosgrave, Minister for Local Government, and his young assistant, Kevin O'Higgins, had been taking over the functions of the existing Local Government Board, from which most local authorities had cut themselves off, despite the consequent loss of grant-aid. The new, youthful councils had begun to rid local government of indolence and graft and were working for the welfare of the people. Robert Barton had established a Land Bank, making loans to farmers to enable them to purchase their land, and a Land Commission to work out fairer methods of land purchase.

Land arbitration courts had been set up, developing from more general arbitration courts the first of which began operations in West Clare in 1919. From these came a whole system of parish courts, district courts and even a supreme court in Dublin. They operated successfully in many areas and even Unionists resorted to them. With the RIC bottled up in their barracks or pursuing will o' the wisp Volunteers, normal police duties were often taken over by the IRA themselves.

All in all, though conditions were chaotic, the Dáil administration was certainly more effective than the Castle's. Arthur Griffith, who had prepared a detailed blueprint whilst imprisoned in Gloucester, had good reason to be pleased, the more so since now Lloyd George was making peace overtures.

In December 1920, the Government of Ireland Act, the 'Partition Act', became law. The Lloyd George government hoped that eventually the two parts of Ireland would come together; in addition to the

Council of Ireland 'bridge', the act provided for the fusion of the two parliaments should both vote for it. But the bridge was never built and, even before the act was passed, the boundary had begun to 'harden into permanence', as frontiers, Lloyd George was later to observe, tend to do.

In the summer of 1920 there were serious disturbances in Londonderry and Belfast. Hundreds of Catholic workmen were driven from the Belfast shipyards and mobs burned Catholic houses and took Catholic lives. There was retaliation by the IRA, and in August the Dáil decided to impose a boycott on Belfast goods. Griffith opposed this on the ground that it was directed at part of their own country; it would be a recognition of partition. He yielded to the majority and the boycott, rigorously policed by the IRA, damaged commerce both in Belfast and Dublin. The rift between Catholic-nationalists and Protestant-Unionists widened.

Shortly after Griffith's arrest, he received in Mountjoy an emissary from Lloyd George, Archbishop Clune of Perth. The Archbishop had already met Collins an achievement which must have stunned the British who had put a price of £10,000 on Collins's head. To his duties of Minister of Finance and Adjutant-General, Director of Organisation and Director of Intelligence of the IRA, Collins had now added that of Acting President of the Dáil. Through intermediaries, negotiations went on throughout December but broke down because Lloyd George insisted that the IRA surrender their arms and was not prepared to allow all members of the Dáil to meet freely. He suggested that Collins and Mulcahy, the IRA's tireless and meticulous Chief of Staff, disappear for a while. These conditions were not truce but surrender, Griffith told Archbishop Clune. In the House of Commons, even while he was half-extending an olive branch to the Dáil, Lloyd

George was increasingly belligerent, but some newspapers, influential churchmen and others were swinging public opinion against the bloody campaign in Ireland.

At Christmas, de Valera returned to Dublin and Griffith was relieved that the reins were safely in his hands again. No doubt he would be more successful than Griffith in reducing tension in the Dáil cabinet. Brugha had shown sustained hostility towards Collins; so had Austin Stack, to whom Griffith had handed over his own portfolio of Home Affairs in August. Of Griffith himself Brugha was often contemptuous. 'We are fighters and you have no standing among us,' he was wont to say.[6]

Perhaps to ease these tensions, one of de Valera's first proposals after his return was to post Collins to America. It was a curious decision and Collins declined to go. De Valera may have believed, too, that with Collins out of the way the British might be more amenable; certainly the British saw in de Valera a more congenial leader with whom to negotiate, since he had no responsibility for the murderous outrages they alleged against Collins. Orders were given that de Valera was not to be arrested.

Appalled by the suffering of his people, and desiring a more heroic victory than any which could be won by gunmen, de Valera suggested to the Dáil, in January 1921, a 'lightening' of the IRA effort. He advocated more conventional operations, occasional attacks on a relatively large scale, allied with intense political activity. Receiving little support, he quickly realised that he was out of touch. The war entered its final, dark phase, but light glimmered uncertainly on the horizon.

Retaliation and reprisal went viciously on. More plain clothes detectives were brought into Dublin and Collins countered by forming an Active Service

Unit – a larger Squad – of full-time gunmen. In the
[94] country, the flying columns continually refined their tactics. Little quarter was given. Martial law was extended; there were executions in Cork and Dublin. In February, Brigadier-General Crozier, commanding the Auxiliaries, resigned and made public his disgust with government policy. As if to confirm his allegations, on 7 March the Mayor of Limerick was shot dead. In March, too, Sean MacEoin, one of the most successful guerrilla leaders, and as chivalrous as he was valiant, was badly wounded and captured. A spectacular attempt, led by Emmet Dalton, to rescue him from Mountjoy failed and only the Truce saved him from the gallows.

Elections for the Northern parliament took place on 19 May. Inevitably, the built-in majority of Unionists prevailed. They won forty of fifty-two seats. Sinn Féin candidates, including Griffith, Collins and de Valera, won six seats. Five days later, the twenty-six counties went to the polls, ostensibly to elect the Southern parliament, but the electoral machinery facilitated the election of the second Dáil. The Dáil was to be enlarged, as the Government of Ireland Act provided for 128 members of the proposed Southern parliament. In theory, Dáil Éireann included elected members for all constituencies in the whole of Ireland, but no one was surprised that the Unionists failed to answer the roll-call.

The day appointed for the opening of the Southern parliament was 28 June, but the act provided for its dissolution if less than half the members attended. In that event, the British government intended to impose Crown Colony rule and to extend martial law from 12 July. But they were anxious that this situation should not arise and behind the scenes the movement towards peace gathered momentum. In the British cabinet there was no unanimity on the vexed question of a surrender of arms. Dr (later Viscount) Addison declared that 'no offer of a truce would be worth making unless it were frank and generous in its terms and unaccompanied by harrassing or ambiguous restrictions'.[7] Alfred (Andy) Cope, Assistant Under-Secretary, who had gone to such lengths to understand the Irish point of view that he was accused of delving in the 'Sinn Féin sewers', worked indefatigably to prepare the ground for a settlement.

Griffith had various visitors in Mountjoy and in March put out a statement to the effect that any peace proposals 'should be addressed, not to the Government's prisoners, but to Dáil Éireann'. Although he could take no active part in the Dáil cabinet, Griffith was in constant touch and continued to think and plan ahead. International recognition of Ireland's case was vital and Griffith had some inkling of Lloyd George's fear of United States intervention. He drafted, for the Dáil's consideration, *An Address to the Elected Representatives of Other Nations.*

On 21 April, Lord Derby paid an unofficial but fruitless visit to de Valera. Later, Sir James Craig met de Valera in Dublin to try to find common ground, but it was a case of rock meeting rock. Earlier in the month, the irrepressible Tom Barry had ambushed a British force at Crossbarry and killed thirty-nine. But the IRA lost five lives when they attacked and burned the Custom House in Dublin, creating chaos by the destruction of records – which would have been useful one day to Ireland's own government – and vandalising one of the finest buildings in the city.

Suddenly, the breakthrough came. King George V, who had long abhorred his government's policy, opened the Northern parliament on 22 June. Inspired by the great South African leader, Field Marshal Smuts, he made a moving plea for peace. In the South it was seen as further evidence that Lloyd George was an-

xious for a settlement and resolve was strengthened.
[96] The British Prime Minister had no fear of military defeat but the moral ground on which he was standing was crumbling. Taking his cue from the King's speech, he sent a letter, much toned down by Churchill and other members of his cabinet, proposing a meeting in London. After consulting with Southern Unionist leaders, de Valera accepted.

On 30 June, Griffith, Mac Néill and Duggan were released from Mountjoy and Griffith had an all too brief respite with his family. He was one of the Irish leaders who met General Macready on 8 July to settle details of a truce. Macready was cheered by a joyous crowd as he arrived at the Mansion House. A truce was signed, to take effect from noon, Monday, 11 July. Recording the meeting in his memoirs, Macready described Griffith as 'a square, squat figure, rather huddled up in his chair, hardly uttering a word, and then only a monosyllable, in whose eyes one could read nothing of what might be passing through his mind.' He added: 'During that hour I understood how it was that Arthur Griffith became a great leader of the Irish.'

So Eamon de Valera went to London, taking with him Griffith, Barton, Stack, Count Plunkett and Erskine Childers. De Valera respected Childers's judgement and often sought his advice, but Griffith regarded him as an Englishman who had espoused the Irish cause rather late in life and who was, like many converts, a zealot.

At a series of four meetings, de Valera and Lloyd George skirmished around their respective positions. The Irish leader spoke at tedious length, exasperating Lloyd George, who thought nevertheless that he had 'an agreeable personality'. The gap between them was wide. De Valera insisted that only a republic would be acceptable to the people of Ireland. The British

Prime Minister offered dominion status, with certain limitations. At least it was an advance on the Home Rule measure of 1914 and Arthur Griffith began to take hope.

Sir James Craig issued a statement in which he urged that the six counties also had a right to self-determination. De Valera was angry but not to be budged. Some measure of local autonomy could be agreed, he intimated, but the unity of the country must be preserved. Lloyd George was convinced that both Craig and de Valera wanted a settlement but were afraid of their respective supporters. He had to move warily himself, lest he antagonise the Conservative members of his coalition government. Already they scented concession and were restive. The obstinate refusal of the Ulstermen to accept a single parliament for the whole of Ireland Lloyd George saw as the real problem. Little progress was made but the two leaders edged away whenever their discussion seemed upon the brink of total disagreement. From time to time, the British leader showed the mailed fist, warning de Valera that, if the truce had to be terminated, 'the struggle would have an entirely different character.'[8] There would be a huge influx of troops into Ireland. De Valera was not impressed, but he probably failed to realise that what concerned the British cabinet, perhaps even more than the chink in Britain's armour which a neutral Irish republic would entail, was the danger of setting a precedent which 'might then prove impossible to resist in the case of India'.[9] The future, not of Ireland alone, but of the Empire was at stake.

Rather reluctantly, Lloyd George put the British proposals in writing and the Irish delegation returned with them to Dublin. Although Brugha and Stack wanted to pursue the course of negotiation no further, the cabinet decided to reject the proposals but to leave

the door open. De Valera was confident that they
[98] were not Lloyd George's last word. On 10 August he sent a long reply, based in part on a draft prepared by Childers. It reiterated Ireland's grievances and aspirations and the justice of her cause, and appealed to reason and for a magnanimous approach. It introduced a new concept, tentative as yet, but soon to become the flagstaff of the republican case. It was an alternative to dominion status, yet offered a means by which Ireland would remain within the British sphere of influence. 'A certain treaty of association with the British Commonwealth group, as with a partial league of nations, we would have been ready to recommend, and as a Government to negotiate and take responsibility for, had we an assurance that the entry of the nation as a whole into such association would secure for it the allegiance of the present dissenting minority, to meet whose sentiment alone this step could be contemplated.' De Valera hoped that this concept would placate his own die-hard republicans, reconcile the Unionist minority and reassure the British. It would require concession from each party, but, with good will all round, he believed it was a workable compromise.

The second Dáil was to assemble on 16 August and the British cabinet decided on an amnesty for the thirty-seven members of the Dáil who were in prison. 'For some inscrutable reason,' Macready wrote in his memoirs, 'McKeown alone was debarred from this amnesty by the authorities in London.'[10] Most of the cabinet felt that concession had gone far enough and that MacEoin should hang, but Lloyd George telegraphed from Paris that 'no risk should be taken of jeopardising settlement over this case'.[11] A telegram from Macready finally convinced the cabinet and MacEoin duly took his seat in the Dáil.

Unanimously the Dáil rejected the British proposals.

De Valera gave an account of the stewardship of the underground administration and then, on 26 August, the old government resigned. Proposed by MacEoin, with Mulcahy seconding, de Valera, until now officially *Príomh Aire* or Prime Minister, was elected President of the Republic of Ireland. There was a hidden significance in this. It meant that the Supreme Council of the IRB acknowledged that there was now a properly constituted republic and that the caretaker President, in fact Michael Collins, now renounced his title.

A long and crafty exchange of letters between the President and Lloyd George followed. Throughout, de Valera tried to manoeuvre his adversary into some kind of acknowledgment of Ireland's sovereign, republican government, but Lloyd George was not to be trapped. In the end, the now famous formula devised by Lloyd George, a masterpiece of ambiguity which recognised no entrenched positions, enabled de Valera to accept an invitation to a conference in London, on 11 October, at which the British would meet the Irish delegates 'as spokesmen of the people whom you represent with a view to ascertaining how the association of Ireland with the community of nations known as the British Empire may best be reconciled with Irish National aspirations'.

The President's controversial decision not to lead the delegation himself has been debated ever since. The cabinet, which chose the delegates, was divided. Cosgrave remarked that it was a pity to have 'the best player in the reserves'.[12] But de Valera believed that by remaining in Ireland, where in any case strong leadership was needed as the dichotomy inherent in the Sinn Féin formula of 1917 was becoming all too apparent, he could take a detached view of the negotiations as reported back to him and could more easily detect the sophisms he expected from Lloyd George.

Arthur Griffith was appointed chairman of the

delegation and a most unwilling and unhappy Collins
[100] agreed to go as his deputy. De Valera was afraid that both might prefer the bird in the hand, on the basis that they could look in the bush later, and Robert Barton, an ardent republican, was appointed as a counterweight. Erskine Childers, one of three secretaries – the others were John Chartres and Fionan Lynch – could also be relied upon to keep the Republic well to the forefront. Two lawyers, Eamonn Duggan and George Gavan Duffy, completed the team. On the face of it, Collins was the least likely to yield the Republic, but apparently de Valera had some inkling that he might be prepared to accept dominion status as a first step.[13] Collins was convinced that whatever happened he would be in the wrong. The appointments were confirmed by the Dáil, who gave the delegates plenary powers, but they were also to be subject to cabinet instructions.

7
The Talk of London

A special train had been laid on by the British government to take the Irish delegation from Holyhead to London. Kathleen Napoli McKenna, who was Arthur Griffith's personal secretary, recalled in 1971[1] that they were 'luxuriously ensconced in a spacious compartment hung with reproductions of masterpieces, furnished with deep armchairs, immense Chesterfield divans, writing desks and carpeted with Oriental rugs'. As they passed through Chester, Griffith showed 'intense interest in the Roman walls and vestiges of the Roman occupation of Britain'.

On arrival in London, the plenipotentiaries were warmly received by large crowds and went straight to their quarters, at 22 Hans Place and 15 Cadogan Gardens. A trip to Epping Forest had been arranged for the following day, Sunday, 9 October, and his secretary records that Arthur Griffith 'talked freely and in a happy, unrestrained way which was somewhat of a revelation to me'. With Michael MacWhite, whom he had just appointed Irish Representative in Switzerland, Griffith made a reminiscent visit to Reading where they drove around the jail. Griffith had no wish to go inside again.

Serious business was to begin on Tuesday, 11 October, and at 10 Downing Street crowds of supporters, some of whom knelt in prayer, were waiting for the Irish delegates who, totally inexperienced in negotiation at this level, found themselves facing a

team of some of the greatest political heavyweights
[102] of the day – Lloyd George himself, Lord Birkenhead, Austen Chamberlain, Winston Churchill, Sir Hamar Greenwood and Sir Laming Worthington-Evans. The Attorney-General, Sir Gordon Hewart, stood by. Birkenhead, who liked to have some idea of the opposition beforehand, had had an *aide memoire* prepared for him. Of Griffith it was said: 'Will be historical, probably even more so than de Valera; will start somewhere about AD 1000 and argue up to the sovereign independent right of every nation; will set out to show that Ireland is a nation; usually silent; not a good speaker but said to be a fair conversationalist; will be ill-at-ease; is more clever than de Valera, but not so attractive; is the real power in Sinn Féin.' The astute Birkenhead soon had a more accurate picture of Griffith than that.

After cool introductions, the representatives of the two countries began a wary, probing session. Lloyd George said at once that he and his colleagues were bound by certain limitations as, no doubt, were the Irish delegates. Griffith made it clear that the Irish delegation expected 'a change in the policy of subordinating Ireland to English interests'. There were exploratory discussions on defence, finance and trade and sub-committees were appointed to deal with these matters which were, though not the core of negotiation, important in their own right.

Irish strategy was to ensure that, if the negotiations failed, the break would come on the issue of partition. In pre-conference discussions the British cabinet had seen that this would be 'far less favourable to us than if the break came on the refusal to accept British sovereignty'.[2] On Friday, 14 October, the Ulster question came up for the first time. Lloyd George counselled patience. All the dominions had begun by being divided, he offered. He was sure that the two parts of Ireland would unite, but not if Ulster were forced. Indignantly, Collins refuted the analogy: 'The British have divided an ancient and historic State.' Griffith, awaiting instructions from Dublin, talked out the session. An exasperated Lloyd George told Lord Riddell that 'unfortunately he had no power of expression', an impression which Griffith was to put right in the coming weeks.

After the first weekend, with de Valera's brief in his pocket, Griffith played a canny game. His chief suggested that the six Ulster counties should be invited to become once again an integral part of Ireland, sending representatives to a Dublin parliament or, alternatively, subordinating their own parliament to Dublin instead of Westminster. Griffith vouchsafed only that 'a fair proposal' would be made to the North and, if no arrangement were agreed, the people should be allowed to choose. Lloyd George was amenable. The border was 'a compromise reached as the result of negotiations with previous representatives of Southern Ireland', he said, not without a hint of mischief, and Britain would endorse any effort to persuade the North to come in, short of force.

The course of the negotiations was jolted when the Pope telegraphed King George V to wish the conference a successful outcome. In his reply the King referred to 'my people', which aroused de Valera's ire. In a long telegram to the Pope, he stated Ireland's case and made it clear that the people of Ireland did not owe allegiance to the British King. Lloyd George erupted; de Valera had made negotiations almost impossible. Griffith and his colleagues, also displeased, cooled the Prime Minister's apparent anger. Apparent because every move Lloyd George made had been rehearsed at meetings of the British representatives. There was nothing new in the arguments de Valera

had put to the Pope; he had been putting the same
[104] arguments to Lloyd George for months.

Now, emphasising the political risks his government were taking, Lloyd George demanded an answer to three fundamental questions. Was Ireland prepared to belong to the Empire, to swear allegiance to the King and to provide defence facilities? The incident had enabled him to swing the argument away from partition, back to the Crown, but Griffith had no intention of breaking on that issue. Apart from playing into British hands, it would mean that a united country was a lost cause. For nearly twenty years he had held to his advocacy of a dual monarchy for the one reason that the Unionists would never withdraw allegiance to the Crown. But he had his instructions and skilfully he stuck to his brief.

On Monday, 24 October, Griffith tabled the Irish proposals. The document mentioned neither Republic nor Crown: 'On the one hand, Ireland will consent to adhere for all purposes of agreed concern to the League of Sovereign States associated and known as the British Commonwealth of Nations. On the other hand, Ireland calls upon Great Britain to renounce all claims to authority over Ireland and Irish affairs.' On the partition issue the proposal was unambiguous: 'The responsibility for this unnatural and indefensible dismemberment rests with the British Government, but as the fact exists we propose to deal with it in the first instance by meeting the elected representatives of our countrymen in the area and forming an agreement with them safeguarding any lawful interests peculiar to the area. Should we fail to come to an agreement, and we are confident we shall not fail, then freedom of choice must be given to electorates within the area.'

Implicit in the last sentence was recognition that the Irish might have to concede partition in some form, regaining perhaps some part of the six-county area. It seemed that de Valera and his cabinet members in Dublin were making the Crown the dominant issue. Lloyd George attacked on that issue. Ireland would adhere to the Commonwealth for all purposes of agreed concern? What was meant by that? 'To put it bluntly, will you be British subjects or foreigners? You must be either one or the other,' said Lloyd George as Griffith tried to explain de Valera's concept of external association. Lloyd George was to live to see the concept become the standard pattern of Commonwealth membership, but in that still imperialist era it was a chimerical idea. There was also the consideration that Irish neutrality would make England vulnerable. Griffith reassured the British on that point: 'In principle we accept that your safety should be secured.'

Not too disheartened, Lloyd George arranged a private meeting between himself and Chamberlain on the one hand, Griffith and Collins on the other. From then on, much of the negotiation was conducted in this way, which was much more practical than plenary sessions. Adversaries of Griffith and Collins in the days to come were to hold this against them, alleging that the British had divided the delegation deliberately and chosen their men. Following the meeting Lloyd George neatly encapsulated the Irish position for his colleagues:

1. Irish not to be aliens but there is to be common and interchangeable citizenship.
2. They will come into the mechanism of the Empire and take part in the Empire's common council to discuss common purposes, e.g. defence of British and Irish coast, though they boggle over joining in a war on behalf of the Dominions.
3. They agree in principle that British Govern-

ment should occupy their ports for Imperial defence
[106] even if the exercise of that right involved war.
They do not however accept the Crown. The head
of state would be chosen by them.

The Prime Minister was convinced that in the end the Irish would accept the Crown, provided Ulster could be brought in. Griffith had said, 'If we came to an agreement on all other points I could recommend some form of association with the Crown.' That was not quite the same thing, but when Griffith reported this, as he reported every day, de Valera scented danger and warned that there could be no question of allegiance to the King, even if the alternative was war. The plenipotentiaries protested that Dublin was inhibiting their powers 'to range freely in discussion' and pointed out that any association with the Commonwealth implied recognition of its head. John Chartres suggested that recognition in this sense subtracted nothing from the ideal of a republic.

Lloyd George told his colleagues that the only way the Irish could be persuaded to accept the Crown was to secure Irish unity. This was not to deny Ulster autonomy. Hewart and Chamberlain, deputed to meet Griffith and Collins privately, reported that they had given satisfactory assurances that the rights of the minority would be safeguarded but they were 'inexorable that they must not leave homogeneous Catholic areas in Ulster'. They were evidently envisaging autonomy to a reduced area and had been told that, whilst the British government could not abandon the 1920 Act, they would do their best to recommend inclusion of the six counties in an all-Ireland parliament, their own parliament to remain autonomous but subordinate to Dublin. Griffith informed de Valera that the plenipotentiaries thought this new proposal 'might be a possible basis', but they had kept that to themselves.

Fresh sets of proposals in writing continued to be exchanged and the Irish girl secretaries slogged unendingly at these and the masses of supporting papers and correspondence. Griffith was solicitous of their welfare and saw to it that in the evenings they were entertained. Once, at Hans Place, he complained, 'Where is that fellow Childers? He is always writing memoranda that aren't wanted, and he can't be found to take the girls to the theatre.'[3]

In his own leisure moments Griffith went for long walks in London, or to the theatre, where he enjoyed Gilbert and Sullivan. Sometimes there were musical evenings at Hans Place such as he had enjoyed so often in Dublin. He had 'a sweet, weak singing voice', according to Kathleen McKenna.

Lloyd George was to face a vote of censure in the Commons on 31 October and Tom Jones, the Cabinet Assistant Secretary, arranged a meeting at Churchill's home on the evening before. The Prime Minister asked for the plenipotentiaries' support in his struggle against the die-hards in the Commons. Griffith reported to de Valera that Lloyd George and Birkenhead had indicated that 'if they were certain of real goodwill on our side they would take risks and fight.' Having survived the censure debate with ease, Lloyd George explained that the next hurdle was the Unionist conference at Liverpool on 17 November. At the same time it would present an opportunity to try to move the stubborn Craig faction. He wanted Griffith to put on paper the assurances given verbally at Churchill's home on 30 October. Griffith drafted a letter which he proposed to send in his own name. Barton and Gavan Duffy suspected a trap and rightly held that any such document should be signed by all the plenipotentiaries. Gavan Duffy was convinced that 'the main effect of the letter must be to undermine the stand we have taken.' A modified letter was delivered personally by Griffith and Collins to Birkenhead.

[108] Arriving in London on 5 November, James Craig was dismayed to find the six counties had been used as a bargaining counter. He would have nothing to do with any proposal which altered the status quo and was unmoved when Lloyd George pleaded that he would be accused of breaking faith with the plenipotentiaries and might even be compelled to resign. Craig's attitude was explained to Griffith by Tom Jones, who added that Lloyd George would make one more attempt to soften Craig and would resign if he failed. That would mean a government led by Bonar Law, who was anything but friendly to Sinn Féin. Lloyd George's resignation threat, so often uttered and forgotten, may have been genuine. It is not mentioned in cabinet records but he did tell Lord Riddell, 'I am not going to continue the Irish war if a settlement is possible. I shall resign and the King will have to send for someone else.' The threat did not trouble Griffith. Whoever was in power in England would have the same problem to face. Just the same, the responsibility and the stress of the negotiations had told on Griffith, immeasurably helped by Collins though he was. No longer light-hearted, he looked older and ill.

A few days later, Jones called again. Would Griffith support the idea of a Boundary Commission, the purpose of which, Griffith explained to de Valera, was to delimit the six-county area 'so as to give us the districts in which we are a majority'? He went on, 'We said it was their proposal not ours and we would therefore not be bound by it, but we realise its value as a tactical manoeuvre and if Lloyd George made it we would not queer his position.' Griffith had been careful, but not subtle enough. In effect, he had recognised the Boundary Commission as a workable alternative.

Churchill and Chamberlain now drafted a memorandum to Craig, putting the onus on the six counties to [109]
avert the reconquest of Ireland, which would be necessary if statesmanship could find no alternative. The real need was peace, not 'a wasted and blood-stained wilderness'. Sinn Féin would probably accept the Crown, provided the Northern parliament became subordinate to Dublin. 'It is no answer to say that Southern Ireland is alone to blame for the present position and that these concessions are offered as the reward of rebellion,' Craig, who obviously had argued on those lines, was warned. The Ulsterman was not intimidated. Refusing to consider an all-Ireland parliament, the subordination of the Northern parliament or any tampering with the border, he suggested instead that if the South were to become a dominion so too could the North. One day, an all-Ireland parliament might be practicable, in which case the machinery of the 1920 act would suffice.

Lloyd George refused to consider this. 'Such a partition must militate with increasing force against the ultimate unity of Ireland,' he replied prophetically. Tom Jones visited Griffith on the morning of 12 November and Lloyd George saw him in the afternoon. At the Liverpool conference Craig would be made a further offer—an all-Ireland parliament, with Ulster having the right to vote itself out within twelve months but, in that event, submitting to a Boundary Commission.

Arthur Griffith now made the error of an honest man who believes that other men are as honest as he. He told Lloyd George that he could not guarantee to accept the proposal but would not embarrass him by repudiating it. He had already given the idea of a Boundary Commission tacit approval. As Conservative ministers in Lloyd George's coalition government, Chamberlain and Birkenhead were to attend the Liver-

pool conference, and Lloyd George 'had no intention
[110] of asking them to embark on an enterprise which, even if ultimate settlement resulted, might smash their political careers, unless he felt sure that he could rely on Griffith not to let him down'.[4] Chamberlain understood from Lloyd George that Griffith would not force a break on the Ulster issue *at any stage.* Griffith even initialled a note drafted by Lloyd George which repeated that if Ulster refused to join an all-Ireland parliament, 'it would be necessary to revise the boundaries of Northern Ireland', that 'this might be done by a Boundary Commission which would be directed to adjust the line both by inclusion and exclusion so as to make the boundary conform as closely as possible to the wishes of the population'.

On 16 November, the British presented a draft of the terms they were now prepared to offer, including the Ulster solution. The Crown was not specifically mentioned, but Ireland was to be a self-governing dominion. The Irish took heart; the draft did not appear to preclude an externally associated republic. The plenipotentiaries were advised by de Valera to submit fresh proposals, 'as far as possible our final word'. When a 'Memorandum by the Irish Representatives' was drafted, Griffith and Childers argued heatedly. Childers thought too much had been conceded. The formula used this time embodied Chartres's phrase recognising the Crown as 'the symbol and accepted head of the Association'. The 'essential unity' of Ireland was a prerequisite but no mention was made of a Boundary Commission. Lloyd George felt the negotiations had got nowhere. Somehow Tom Jones and Griffith held the conference together and Griffith explained to de Valera that, unless Ireland would come into the Empire, there was no hope of any agreement with Craig on Ulster.

At an acrimonious meeting on 23 November, Griffith, Collins and Barton covered every angle with Lloyd George, Birkenhead and Chamberlain and saw no agreement. Birkenhead, who throughout had most impressed the Irish representatives, was conciliatory, but Lloyd George was in belligerent mood as he tried to drive the conference to a climax. He wanted an answer by the next day when he was to meet Craig. Imperturbably Griffith repeated that they would agree to the Ulster proposals if Ulster did. The Prime Minister was satisfied on this point but demanded complete agreement on the Crown.

The following day, Birkenhead and Hewart met Griffith, Collins, Gavan Duffy and Chartres, and Chartres put it bluntly that External Association meant the Crown would have no significance within Ireland. Hewart summed up the Irish argument in an *aide memoire*. 'Powers which existed in theory might be of little account in relation to distant Dominions. They would appear much more real to the Irish people, and in relation to Ireland ought not even in name exist.' Griffith determinedly carried on the argument for external association though he would happily have accepted the Crown. It was a tense meeting and Hewart threw away Lloyd George's trump card as he sought to reassure the Irish delegates. They 'must not suppose the British Government was contemplating the alternative of war'. Hastily Lloyd George recovered his ace, sending a note purporting to confirm what Hewart had said. It read: 'The Irish delegates must not suppose that the British Government was contemplating with equanimity the alternative which was war.'

The plenipotentiaries returned to Dublin to discuss the position with the cabinet. Other delegates had made several trips to Ireland during the negotiations but this was the first time Griffith had returned home. He and de Valera discussed the course of the negotia-

tions as they drove in the Dublin hills, a drive which
[112] could not have given Griffith much relaxation. After the cabinet meeting, on 25 November, the delegates returned to London with an agreed memorandum which Griffith reinforced with a well-reasoned note of his own. He denied Britain's claim that Ireland was being offered the same status as Canada. Ireland would not control her own defence and she was required to make bases available to Britain. This latter was not a point that Ireland wished to quarrel about, but it did illustrate Griffith's contention. On the question of allegiance there was a practical difference if not a theoretical one. For distant Canada the Crown really was just a symbol but, because Ireland was on Britain's doorstep, the Crown would 'continue to possess the real power of repression and veto which Ireland knows'.

Lloyd George's answer, given at a late night meeting at Chequers, 'knocked out my argument', Griffith reported to de Valera. He simply invited the Irish to choose any phrase which would satisfy them that the constitutional function of the Crown would be the same in Ireland as in Canada. The British Prime Minister now injected a sense of urgency into the negotiations. Craig had been promised the British proposals by 6 December. Perhaps because he added encouragingly that he had begged Craig 'seriously to consider' whether the six counties would not be better off inside an all-Ireland parliament, the Irish representatives apparently accepted the deadline without question. Exhausted as they were by week upon week of hard bargaining, they may well have lacked the will to protest. Lloyd George was to let Griffith have a copy of the proposals by 1 December.

In the Belfast parliament Craig announced on 29 November: 'By Tuesday next these negotiations will have broken down or the Prime Minister will send me new proposals for consideration by the cabinet. In the meantime, the rights of Ulster will be in no way [113] sacrificed or compromised.' His statement had been agreed with Lloyd George and must have been a stratagem to bring the negotiations to a close.

Tom Jones delivered the redrafted Articles of Agreement late on 30 November and there was further discussion on the following two days. Amendments were made but a form of Oath suggested by the Irish was not accepted. Nevertheless, much ground had been won in the week and Griffith believed they had reached the end of the road. It would be difficult to reconcile the doctrinaire republicans at home to the terms, but he was well aware that Lloyd George's coalition government was also under strain. If it were to break, there would be no hope of gaining similar terms from a Conservative government and a resumption of the war would be all too likely.

Copies of the latest draft Articles were given by Jones to Childers, who remained with Collins to iron out some creases in the financial arrangements, while Griffith set off for Dublin. Griffith travelled with Duggan and John (later Mr Justice) O'Byrne. They went carefully through the draft Treaty, which Griffith was carrying in an ancient attaché case. Griffith remarked that the clause dealing with the boundary would make the position of the North quite untenable.[5] He was convinced that any reassessment of the border would mean the South would get most of Tyrone and Fermanagh and areas of County Down and Armagh. O'Byrne thought too much was left to the Boundary Commission and suggested a plebiscite with specified electoral areas which would go to one side of the line or the other, according to the majority. Griffith 'immediately saw the point but said he did not know whether it would be possible at that stage to have it altered'.[6]

Collins, Gavan Duffy and Childers took a later
[114] boat, were involved in a collision and had to return to Holyhead. They were very weary when they arrived for the cabinet meeting on 3 December. It was a turbulent day, with Brugha and Stack so insistent on a republic that the much more important question of national unity became a secondary issue. De Valera thought Griffith had achieved neither independence nor national unity, and declared that the terms must be drastically amended, even if stalemate meant war. It was at this meeting that Brugha first made the barbed comment that the British government had 'selected its men'.

A suggestion that de Valera himself should go to London was not pursued when Griffith gave an assurance that he would attempt to secure amendments and would not sign the Agreement but would bring it back for the Dáil and, if necessary, the people to consider it. Gavan Duffy, Duggan and Childers, who were not in the cabinet, and Kevin O'Higgins, Assistant Minister for Finance, joined the meeting. The Oath was discussed. De Valera, who saw no need for an Oath at all, proposed:

> I do solemnly swear true faith and allegiance to the Constitution of the Irish Free State, to the Treaty of Association, and to recognise the King of Great Britain as Head of the Association.

This was better than Lloyd George's, if only as a piece of literature, G. B. Shaw commented.

Cathal Brugha remarked presciently that the proposed Agreement would 'split Ireland from top to bottom'. The cabinet, and the delegation itself, were already bitterly divided. Griffith insisted that these were the best terms possible. Duggan agreed and Collins, in a very unhappy frame of mind, was also inclined to agree. Gavan Duffy and Barton thought Lloyd George was bluffing, and Childers, with whom Griffith had become more and more testy in London, was coldly and implacably against acceptance.

In two hostile parties the delegation returned to London and the rift was quickly perceived by Lloyd George. The plenipotentiaries were not even sure of their instructions, which was nothing new, for at various times during the negotiations they seemed not to have been adequately briefed. The notes taken at the ill-tempered cabinet meeting by the acting secretary, Colm Ó Murchadha, seem clear. The plenipotentiaries were to refuse the Oath unless it were amended, were not to sign the Agreement on the grounds that it should be accepted by the Dáil. Should there be stalemate, they were to ensure that the break came on the Ulster issue.

In London the argument with the British team was resumed but, as Griffith tried to make Ulster the key issue, Gavan Duffy admitted, 'Our difficulty is to come into the Empire, looking at all that has happened in the past.' His words snapped the patience of Chamberlain and Lloyd George. 'In that case, it's war,' said the Prime Minister, bringing the meeting to an end. The Irish were to send a formal rejection. But Tom Jones persuaded a reluctant Collins to see Lloyd George, who was convinced that Griffith, despite his brave arguments, had been won over and that Collins was hesitating.

Early in the morning of 5 December, Collins and Lloyd George went over all the ground again to little avail. Afterwards, according to C. P. Scott, Lloyd George was excited and angry. The Irish had 'gone back on everything'.[7] Yet the Prime Minister gave his cabinet a cool and careful resumé of the situation, which he blamed on de Valera and his colleagues in Ireland. There was general agreement that the Oath

could be modified but that recognition of the King in
[116] Ireland was essential.

At 3 p.m. the same day, Griffith, Collins and Barton faced Lloyd George, Churchill, Chamberlain and Birkenhead. A quite warm relationship had developed between Birkenhead and Collins. Of all the English negotiators Birkenhead had been the one who seemed best able to understand the Irish viewpoint. Griffith, with little hope now of salvaging the negotiations, and anxious to force the break on Ulster, took the line Collins had taken in the morning. If Ulster would come in, he would accept inclusion in the Empire. At the last minute, Lloyd George remembered the document casually initialled by Griffith on 12 November. After a search it was found in his wardrobe and he was able to produce it and, rather theatrically, accuse Griffith of going back on his word. Had he not already agreed to the alternative of a Boundary Commission? It broke Griffith. He had believed that the document confirmed only that he would not repudiate the proposal Lloyd George intended his Conservative Ministers to make at the Liverpool Conference. But the note could be construed to mean that he accepted the proposal as an alternative to unity and, indeed, Lloyd George had intended that. He had advised Chamberlain at the time that that was the understanding. Griffith had forgotten the note; his colleagues did not even know it existed.

Griffith could bear no dent in the impregnable armour of his honour. 'I said I would not let you down on that and I won't,' he growled. Now he could break on neither the Empire nor Ulster. Lloyd George may or may not have been devious but he took full advantage of the situation. The question which was so vital to the Irish case could have been put to Craig. The deadline was an arbitrary one and could quite easily have been extended, but the Prime Minister had played a psychological game and it was fixed in the Irish mind that it was now 'make or break'.

At this point, the British delegates conferred in another room and returned with a form of Oath based on a draft submitted by Collins that morning and amended by Birkenhead. Finally incorporated in the Treaty, it read:

> I . . . do solemnly swear true faith and allegiance to the Constitution of the Irish Free State as by law established, and that I will be faithful to HM King George V, his heirs and successors by law, in virtue of the common citizenship of Ireland with Great Britain and her adherence to and membership of the group of nations forming the British Commonwealth of Nations.

Churchill conceded points on defence which only an hour earlier he had insisted upon, the British yielded more ground on trade and also agreed that Ulster should be required to give a decision for or against union with the South within one calendar month of the act being passed.

'We have gone through this document and met you fairly,' said Lloyd George after a further adjournment. 'Are you now prepared to stand by this Agreement whichever choice Ulster makes?'

Only Griffith agreed.

Lloyd George played his last card. He held up the two letters he had prepared for Sir James Craig. Which was he to send? The one which would enclose a copy of the Articles of Agreement, or the other, 'telling Sir James Craig that the Sinn Féin representatives refuse allegiance and refuse to come within the Empire and that I have no proposals to make to him'. If the second letter were to be dispatched, it would mean war within three days.

Griffith took the threat calmly. On the under-

standing that the proposals were put before parliament
[118] as soon as possible, and that arrangements were made to evacuate British troops and establish a provisional government in Ireland, he would do his best to have the Agreement ratified by the Dáil. He emphasised that this was his personal pledge only. Arthur Griffith believed that as a matter of honour he was committed. His colleagues were not. The Prime Minister declared that he was willing to risk the fate of his own government and the Irish delegates should *all* make a decision. The issue, he repeated, was peace or war. He built up an atmosphere of desperate urgency, the train with steam up at Euston, the impatient destroyer waiting at Holyhead, the messenger Mr (later Sir Geoffrey) Shakespeare in readiness. . . . 'If he is to reach Sir James Craig in time, we must know your answer by 10 p.m. tonight.' The plenipotentiaries did not ask, 'In time for what?', nor did they question the significance of Craig's bogey-man role. Perhaps they did not need to, but accepted it for what it was, a piece of stage machinery designed to bring the negotiations to a climax.

It was already 7.15 p.m. On the way back to their London headquarters, Collins decided to sign. When they reached Hans Place, he took no part in the agonised discussion upstairs but, says Kathleen McKenna,[8] tramped morosely up and down, eventually flinging himself into a chair and falling asleep.

Having come to his decision, Arthur Griffith seemed serious but unperturbed, Eamonn Duggan was overwhelmed by the thought that the war might be renewed, that the weary Irish people, transparently relieved by the truce, would, without any choice in the matter themselves, have to draw on fresh reserves of energy, patience and courage. He decided to cast in his lot with Griffith and Collins. Robert Barton and George Gavan Duffy, loath to disown the Republic and settle for dominion status and allegiance to the Crown, in the end agreed there was no alternative.

Whether or not the British government would have carried out the threat of war has often been argued. Certainly they would have received little encouragement from the British people. But there was no question of Ireland's being allowed off the Empire hook; when in April 1922, it was feared that an attempt would be made to overthrow the Provisional Government set up under the provisions of the Treaty and to establish an Irish Republican government, it was agreed by the British cabinet that 'the mere fact of its being brought into being would constitute a state of war between it and the British Empire'.[9] Elaborate plans to deal with such an emergency were made and there is no reason to think that had the Treaty negotiations failed, the British would have taken a different course.

The Irish team had been at a disadvantage from the outset, not only because they lacked the experience and aplomb of their adversaries, but because they had such long lines of communication to their colleagues. The British could consult their cabinet colleagues or draw on the expertise of their civil servants at very short notice. They were negotiating, too, from a position of historic strength in Ireland. It was no surprise that the British won a tactical victory in bringing the conference to an end but they had been pushed to the very limit of concession. For Arthur Griffith perhaps the most important concession was that of full fiscal powers, gained almost at the last minute. Control of the purse-strings would give Ireland an enormous advantage when eventually further negotiations were embarked upon, as both Griffith and Collins believed inevitably they would be.

The ten o'clock deadline was long past before the uncomfortable decision to sign the Treaty document

finally was made. But Lloyd George waited. So did
[120] Mr Shakespeare and his train at Euston and the destroyer at Holyhead. Griffith, Collins and Barton returned to 10 Downing Street immediately.

'Mr Prime Minister, the delegation is willing to sign the Agreements, but there are a few points of drafting which perhaps it would be convenient if I mentioned at once,'[10] said Arthur Griffith. Minor amendments were made and at 2.10 a.m. on 6 December 1921, the Treaty was signed.

Much has been made of the delegation's extraordinary failure to telephone de Valera and seek last-minute guidance. There is probably no single explanation. De Valera, they knew, was in Limerick and it might have been difficult to get through to him, but apparently they did not even try, and it would seem that even Childers did not suggest it. The tremendous sense of urgency created by Lloyd George was probably the main factor in persuading the plenipotentiaries to go ahead without reference to their President. Plausible, too, is Colum's suggestion that they were expecting opposition from Brugha and Stack but not from de Valera himself.[11] If he had not been prepared to accept compromise, why had he sent the delegation to London in the first place?

Richard Mulcahy, who was in Limerick with de Valera, took a telephone call from Gearóid O'Sullivan a few hours after the signing of the Treaty. 'They are after signing,' said O'Sullivan and Mulcahy passed on the news. 'I did not think they would give in so soon', was de Valera's famous but enigmatic response. He did not say whom he meant by 'they'.

8
Ideals in Conflict

The President returned to Dublin, where he had an evening engagement, and first saw the terms of the Agreement in the newspapers. Shortly afterwards, Duggan and Desmond Fitzgerald arrived with the copy of the Agreement and, not surprisingly, got a cool reception. Unaware that the newspapers already carried the news, Duggan informed de Valera that the text was to be published in the late editions. 'What, to be published whether I have seen it or not – whether I have approved it or not,'[1] exclaimed the indignant de Valera.

Sean Milroy, who saw Griffith as he was leaving Hans Place, with his wife, to get the train to Holyhead, thought there was 'an air of immeasurable weariness about him'. But, when Griffith spoke, 'there was a note, not of elation, but of calm, inflexible decision'.[2]

Michael Collins was satisfied that he had done the right thing but was pessimistic as to the outcome. In a letter to John O'Kane, penned while he was still in London, he wrote: 'Think – what have I got for Ireland? Something which she has wanted these past seven hundred years. Will anyone be satisfied at the bargain? Will anyone? I tell you this – early this morning I signed my death warrant.'[3] Succinctly he stated his conviction: 'These signatures are the first real step for Ireland. If people will only remember that, the first real step." This was to be his theme when h defended the Treaty in the Dáil.

Whether the plenipotentiaries had signed the Treat or not, the Dáil had still to ratify it. Had the vot gone against it, the Treaty would have been scrapped whatever the consequences. Even the British wer aware that it was no *fait accompli*, although they wer confident, as Griffith was confident, that it was accep table to the Irish people. Yet de Valera, Brugha, Stack Childers and other opponents of the Treaty reacted a if the action of the delegation in signing was irrever sible. It could perhaps be claimed that, unsigned, th Agreement was more likely to have been thrown ou or, at the very least, that further concessions woul have been demanded. The mind boggles at the though of what a 'committee' of all 121 Dáil Deputies woul have made of the document.

That de Valera did not regard the signatures as fina is evident from his reference to 'the *proposed* treat with Great Britain' in a statement he issued, on December, following a meeting of the cabinet mem bers still in Dublin. At that meeting he had announce that he would demand the resignations of Griffith Collins and Barton but had been persuaded by Cos grave that he should hear their explanations first. Th offending plenipotentiaries were summoned by tele gram to a cabinet meeting at noon on Thursday 8 December. The President's statement was to inforn the people of his action, which was to enable a ful cabinet decision to be taken. The Dáil also was to b convened.

Arthur Griffith returned to Ireland confident that with the President's support, he could rout the oppon ents of the Treaty. That he did not have de Valera' support he learned from Desmond Fitzgerald, one o only three people to welcome him and Mrs Griffit when they stepped off the boat. Surprised at th

President's opposition, Fitzgerald had remarked to Austin Stack, 'I did not think he was against this kind of settlement before he went to London,' and was told, 'He's dead against it now, anyway.'[4] As Fitzgerald passed on the remark to him, Griffith must have wondered just how communication between de Valera and himself had broken down. It may have been that de Valera, influenced by the hard-line republicans, Brugha and Stack, had gradually come to take a less moderate line than he had, for instance, at a secret session of the Dáil on 22 August when he declared that if Britain would accept a republic he 'would be in favour of giving each county power to vote itself out of the Republic if it so wishes'.[5] He had further stated that he was not committed to any particular form of government but would do what he thought best for the country. That was to be the policy of his cabinet, too, and any member who disagreed with him could resign. At various times he denied that he was a 'doctrinaire republican' and he had once begged Griffith to get him out of 'the strait-jacket of the Republic'.

It would be easy to accept that de Valera's attitude seemed to Griffith to have hardened, were it not for the fact that they had recently spent an afternoon together and, only three days before the Treaty was signed, had argued the whole thing through in cabinet. Though Griffith never was convinced by the External Association concept, he argued the case for it stubbornly and skilfully, but he could not believe that the President saw it as a principle for which he was prepared to spend Irish lives. Towards the end of the conference which followed the cabinet meeting on 3 December, Childers had asked if de Valera still insisted upon External Association, from which it can be inferred that the subject had not been discussed. Apparently, Griffith and Collins did not hear

Childers's question, nor de Valera's reply that, yes, he
[124] did insist, and went away convinced that the clause in the draft treaty which would ensure the same status for Ireland as Canada enjoyed had passed muster. Often tortuous in his explanations, de Valera may quite unintentionally have given a weary Griffith the wrong impression.

In London the plenipotentiaries had made strong representations for the immediate release of internees and on 7 December the British cabinet, with the agreement of General Macready who was present, decided to advise the King to act at once to release 4,000 internees as 'it would be more difficult for the Irish Parliament to reject the Articles of Agreement if the internees had been released as an act of clemency immediately after the signature of those articles.'[6]

There was less unanimity in the Irish cabinet, which met the following day and wrangled bitterly about the acceptance of Crown and Empire. The plenipotentiary members of the cabinet were convinced the alternative was war, and perhaps only Collins knew how depleted were the resources of the IRA. Griffith, Collins and Barton, the last still insisting that nothing but the threat of war would have induced him to sign the Treaty, with the support of Cosgrave, narrowly out-voted de Valera, Brugha and Stack. De Valera at once put out a statement which was published in the evening papers that day.

'The terms of this agreement are in violent conflict with the wishes of the majority of the Nation as expressed fully in successive elections during the last three years,' he claimed. He could not recommend acceptance of the Treaty either to Dáil Éireann or to the country and in this he was supported by the Ministers of Home Affairs (Stack) and Defence (Brugha). Exhorting the people to face the crisis 'worthily, without bitterness, and above all, without recriminations,' he added encouragingly: 'There is a definite constitutional way of resolving our political differences,' and he concluded, no doubt with unconscious irony, 'let the conduct of the Cabinet in this matter be an example to the whole nation'.

What the statement did not touch upon was how a renewal of the war with England was to be averted. The people had voted wholeheartedly for Sinn Féin and the republican ideal; they had stood rock-solid behind the IRA; but since the truce had ended the terror, and brought loved ones home, and oiled the springs of rusty businesses, the idea of war for the sake of the difference between dominion status and external association was much more likely to be in violent conflict with the wishes of the people than was the Treaty.

Brugha's prediction that Ireland would be split from top to bottom showed every sign of being fulfilled. Arthur Griffith, returning to his old haunts, seeking out his old cronies, found that not all of them wanted to see him. His twenty-year old friendship with Sean T. O'Kelly ended at this time. O'Kelly was destined to become first President of the Republic of Ireland towards which the first, and largest, step had been taken by Arthur Griffith and Michael Collins.

Before the Treaty debate in the Dáil, which was to assemble on 14 December, Griffith put it to de Valera that as the outcome could be the jettisoning of the Treaty and resumption of hostilities, he should first discuss the position with the GHQ staff of the Army.[7] De Valera called a meeting in the Oak Room of the Mansion House and asked each man whether he could count on his support if the Dáil voted against the Treaty. As Chief of Staff, Mulcahy answered first. He would serve in any capacity de Valera wished, but as a Deputy he would be taking part in the debate and was likely to make certain statements which might well disqualify him from a position of command. He [126] gave it as his opinion that the IRA could sustain a campaign for about six months. Collins replied that he would accept no position of responsibility but would serve as an ordinary soldier. Ironically, it was de Valera, not Collins, who was to become 'a humble soldier'. The other members of the GHQ staff all put themselves at the government's disposal.

The great debate began with quiet formality in the Council Chamber of University College, Dublin, at 11.30 a.m. on Wednesday 14 December 1921. The Speaker, Eoin Mac Néill, was in the chair. Diarmuid O'Hegarty, Clerk of the Dáil, called the roll of Deputies. Prayers were said. There was no indication then of the long, tempestuous sessions which were to come, of the whole range of human emotions that was to be evoked, of magnanimity and meanness, statesmanship and purblind ignorance, generous praise and embarrassing vituperation, all of which were to mark the debate and which, though they must have seemed transient at the time, were painstakingly recorded for posterity. But the printed page can be misleading. The tone of voice, the smile, the raised fist, the shrug of the shoulders, the approving glance or the disapproving silence have no record.

Eamon de Valera began with admirable objectiveness. The Treaty should be considered on its merits. Deputies should not be influenced by 'extraneous matters such as what I might call an accidental division of opinion of the cabinet, or the causes which gave rise to it'. The plenipotentiaries had signed without referring the final text to the cabinet. That was the nub of the argument. Admittedly, the delegates had the power to sign. They were plenipotentiaries of the Dáil, not of the cabinet, but 'I was captaining a team,' he said 'and I felt that the team should have played with me to the last . . .' Griffith denied that the plenipotentiaries had exceeded their instructions. Collins pointed out that, by signing, each delegate had undertaken to recommend the Treaty to the Dáil, and Griffith added that the British Ministers 'had to go to their Parliament and we to ours for ratification'. [127]

Already the sides were taking shape; already there were personal attacks on the plenipotentiaries. The Dáil went into private session. Points of difference could be settled in an hour or so, de Valera estimated, but the private proceedings lasted until the weekend. In the course of them the President put forward an alternative text for a Treaty.

If the Dáil were to embrace this alternative, which became known as Document No. 2, an attempt to re-open negotiations with the British would be attempted. As far as possible, the text reproduced the terms of the Treaty, but there was no oath and no Governor-General; the defence provisions were revised – there would be a definite handing over of coastal defences after five years instead of renegotiation. Fundamentally, it reiterated the External Association case which the British had already flatly rejected. North-East Ulster was covered in an addendum. Although the right of any part of Ireland to be excluded was not admitted, for the sake of internal peace and to make clear that coercion was not intended, the Treaty provisions would be allowed to stand. De Valera had warned the Dáil during a secret session in the previous August that 'if they tried to coerce the North they would be making the same mistake with the majority there that the British had made with the rest of the island.'[8]

Surprisingly, de Valera himself put it that there was very little difference between the Treaty and Document No. 2. He was prepared to fight for that difference; although he described it as 'a little sentimental thing', it was for him the very axle of independence.

He was convinced that Britain would not fight for so
[128] small a difference, but the British equally saw it as fundamental. The common factor was the geographical proximity of the two islands. Despite British assurances that there would be no meddling in Irish affairs, de Valera wanted some extra barrier that Canada, because of distance, did not need to operate an entirely independent dominion. For Britain's part, because sea power was still paramount in those days, she could not risk exposing her vulnerable underbelly by permitting Ireland to become a neutral republic. Promised safeguards were not enough. There was also the fear that India would emulate Ireland's example.

Document No. 2 won little support. Supporters of the Treaty thought it a quibble, a matter almost of semantics, and certainly as much of a compromise as was the Treaty itself. Nor did External Association appeal to those against the Treaty; many fervently desired complete severance of the British connection. Time has proved de Valera's concept practicable, but neither the British nor the Irish of the time saw it as a workable solution.

Withdrawing the document, de Valera insisted that it was not for public discussion. He had put it forward for a distinct purpose, to see whether 'we could get a unanimous proposition by this House'. Griffith and Collins were incensed. De Valera had publicly denounced the Treaty and repudiated them. Now he was not prepared to let the people see how little his own solution varied from the Treaty.

On Monday, 19 December, the Dáil resumed the debate in public and Griffith moved: 'That Dáil Éireann approves of the Treaty between Great Britain and Ireland, signed in London on December 6th, 1921'. He warned that, although he would respect the President's wish as far as he could, he was not going to hide the proposed alternative from the Irish people. He stood before that assembly, in an atmosphere that was tense and simmering with hostility, his small, square figure straight, his hands sometimes betraying the intensity of his own feelings as they fidgetted with his papers, his words delivered earnestly but deliberately in a low key.

The plenipotentiaries had been sent to London 'to reconcile our aspirations with the association of the community of nations known as the British Empire. The task which was given to us was as hard as ever was placed on the shoulders of men.' Others had declined to accept the task but the plenipotentiaries had faced it, aware that whatever the outcome they would have their critics. 'I signed that Treaty,' said Griffith, 'not as the ideal thing, but fully believing, as I believe now, it is a Treaty honourable to Ireland, and safeguards the vital interests of Ireland . . . it is a Treaty of equality, and because of that I am standing by it . . .' It was for the Irish people, 'who are our masters, not our servants as some think', to say whether it was good enough.

He recalled that de Valera had once said he interpreted his oath to the Irish Republic to mean that he was bound to do the best he could for Ireland. The plenipotentiaries had done their best. If it were not enough, if the Irish people said they had everything but the name Republic and would fight for that, 'I would say to them that they are fools, but I will follow in their ranks. . . .' Scathingly he slated those who impugned Michael Collins, 'the man who won the war', by accusing him of compromising Ireland's rights. He pointed out that no demand for a republic had been made in the long correspondence which had led to the negotiations, and claimed that the difference, both in the cabinet and the Dáil, was between 'half recognising the British King and the British Em-

pire and marching in, as one of the speakers put it,
[130] with our heads up'. This was no more than a quibble and, vowed Griffith, 'so far as my power or voice extends not one young Irishman's life shall be lost on that quibble'.

Summing up his own tenacious philosophy, Griffith quoted his lifelong idol, the Young Irelander Thomas Davis: 'Peace with England, alliance with England to some extent, and, under certain circumstances, confederation with England; but an Irish ambition, Irish hopes, strength, virtue, and rewards for the Irish.' Many young Deputies who heard Griffith that day thought him out of touch. For them Davis was a patriot of his time, not a prophet of the twentieth century.

Yet they must have been moved as Griffith went on: 'That is what we have brought back, peace with England, alliance with England, confederation with England, an Ireland developing her own life, carving out her own way of existence, and rebuilding the Gaelic civilisation broken down at the battle of Kinsale.' He asked the Dáil to pass the resolution 'and the Irish people everywhere to ratify this Treaty, to end this bitter conflict of centuries, to end it forever. . . .'

When Sean MacEoin had seconded the motion, Eamon de Valera rose to oppose it. He did so with impressive sincerity. 'A war-weary people will take things which are not in accordance with their aspirations,' he said. Although the people might vote for the Treaty now, ultimately it would not be good enough. He mentioned the document he had presented to the House in private session 'to try to get unanimity'. He believed his alternative would bring peace between peoples and it 'would be consistent with the Irish people being full masters of everything within their shores'.

Michael Collins's address to the Dáil was carefully

thought out, more profound than most. He argued that the real compromise lay in the acceptance of Lloyd George's invitation in the first place. 'If we are stood on the recognition of the Irish Republic as a prelude to any conference we could very easily have said so, and there would be no conference.'

Collins had not abandoned the republican ideal but saw the Treaty as the first stage in its achievement. 'In my opinion,' he declared, 'it gives us freedom, not the ultimate freedom that all nations desire and develop to, but the freedom to achieve it.' He claimed that few understood and appreciated 'the immense powers and liberties it secures'. A very few years later, as he took Ireland step by step towards a republic recognised by all nations, Eamon de Valera acknowledged the truth of Collins's words.

Political freedom was necessary to halt what Collins called the 'slow, steady economic encroach by England'. Only by military strength had the English held Ireland. 'Our aspirations,' he said, 'by whatever term they may be symbolised, had one thing in front all the time, that was to rid the country of the enemy strength.' Collins's new-found pragmatism must have dismayed those for whom nothing but a republic would do and many reacted by calling him traitor, but Collins already had a firm bank of support for, on 10 December, the Supreme Council of the IRB had decided to back ratification.

The republic-or-nothing case was put bluntly by Austin Stack and by Childers, who followed Collins and spoke with dignity and conviction. Cleverly, he introduced external association into his argument but did not push it too hard. It had been perceived already that the opponents of the Treaty might themselves split into two factions. Of the remaining plenipotentiaries Barton declared emotionally that he had broken his oath because it seemed the lesser outrage

forced upon him. Gavan Duffy saw no rational alter-
[132] native to the Treaty. Duggan blamed no threat of war for his signature but had signed deliberately and responsibly. No one could seriously suggest that the plenipotentiaries had been sent to London to ask the British government to recognise the Irish Republic. They had gone to compromise. 'I say under the terms of that Treaty that if the Irish people cannot achieve their freedom it is the fault of the Irish people and not of the Treaty.'

All the principal protagonists had now spoken but everyone wanted a say and had one. Some spoke once and briefly, others at length and several times. Every aspect of the Treaty was hammered at incessantly; old ground was raked over, latent grudges came to the surface. Little was added to the main argument. Less was said about partition than might have been appropriate and, again, Collins took an unexpected line: 'What is the use of talking big phrases about not agreeing to the partition of our country? Surely we recognise that the North East corner does exist, and surely our intention was that we should take such steps as would sooner or later lead to mutual understanding . . . if our policy is, as has been stated, a policy of non-coercion, then let somebody else get a better way out of it.'

On 22 December the Dáil adjourned for Christmas, but in homes and pubs and in the streets the debate went on. Deputies were able to sound public opinion in their constituencies and there were converts from one side to the other in some cases. In the press and from the pulpit there was a steady pressure in favour of the Treaty. On 3 January, the Dáil resumed. What effect the recess had on the outcome of the debate is impossible to say, but it is not unlikely that, had the vote been taken before Christmas, it might have gone de Valera's way. In rather sterile fashion the debate dragged on. Collins suggested the anti-Treaty group might abstain from voting, so absolving their consciences but not the English from their bargain.

Nine Deputies from both parties met at the home of Sean T. O'Kelly and agreed a rather curious proposal: de Valera might advise his followers to abstain, on the understanding that he remain President of the Dáil, from which the Provisional Government should derive its powers and to which it should remain responsible. Recalling the occasion, the late Professor Michael Hayes, one of the nine, reflected that it was 'manifestly absurd that we should agree to keep de Valera on as President and work the Treaty'.[9] De Valera thought so, too, and the idea went no further, though Griffith and Collins found it acceptable.

The Document No. 2 argument lurked beneath the surface throughout and came into the open when Deputy Lorcan Robbins, insisting that there were three parties in the Dáil – the uncompromising Republicans, the Treaty party and the Document No. 2 party – complained that, because the President had vetoed discussion on his alternative, he could not explain to his constituents exactly what the issues were.

De Valera then circulated a modified version of Document No. 2 proposing to put it forward as an amendment to Griffith's original motion. Griffith, who had been exasperated from the beginning that de Valera had not made his alternative public, suggested crisply that it should be given to the press. Although de Valera did not regard the document as confidential, he nevertheless gathered up copies. Griffith, however, smuggled one to the *Freeman's Journal*. De Valera complained but was more exercised by a personal attack which had appeared in the same newspaper and which was deplored by both sides of the House.

On 6 January, in a long speech, de Valera talked of
[134] the difficulty he had had in keeping a balance between the disparate elements in his cabinet as represented by Brugha and Griffith. In 1917 he had become the connecting link between the Sinn Féin organisation and the Volunteers and the two had 'differed then as fundamentally as they differ today'. The President had put his finger on the weakness which his own formula had disguised at the time but for which no one seemed able to find a formula now.

He attempted then, by resigning and offering himself for re-election as soon as Griffith had had his say, to make the issue a vote of confidence in himself. He knew that despite the acrimonious arguments of the long debate, he could draw from a deep well of personal affection and admiration to which the supporters of the Treaty contributed as much as their adversaries. Griffith was not prepared to allow the Dáil to be deflected from consideration of the motion standing in his name. He had listened for days while attacks were made on his honour, he said, and he saw no reason why the discussion should be interrupted by a vote on the personality of President de Valera.

The final day, 7 January, was marred by a vitriolic attack on Collins by Cathal Brugha. 'Bravo, Cathal, bravo,' exclaimed Griffith ironically. Collins, himself, was forbearing. Brugha ended by reversing the abstention idea and pleading with Griffith to abstain. If he were to do so, his name would live for ever in Ireland. Arthur Griffith replied, 'I cannot accept the invitation of the Minister of Defence to dishonour my signature and become immortalised in Irish history.' Defending Collins, he said, 'though I have not now, and never had, an ambition about either political affairs or history, if my name is to go down in history I want it associated with the name of Michael Collins.'

The vote was taken. The Treaty was ratified by

sixty-four votes to fifty-seven. Two days later, de Valera resigned. 'A certain resolution' had been approved, he said, but only the vote of the people could disestablish the Republic. Meanwhile, the Dáil remained the supreme government. Incredibly, de Valera was almost re-elected President, losing by only two votes. Griffith saw no necessity for him to resign. He had suggested already that Dáil Éireann continue until the Free State election. But he regretted that, having resigned, de Valera should stand again. He saw the vote not as against de Valera but 'to help the Treaty'. 'I want to say now that there is scarcely a man I have met in my life that I have more love and respect for than President de Valera. I am thoroughly sorry to see him placed in such a position. We want him with us.'

Promising, 'We will not interfere with you, except when we find that you are going to do something that will definitely injure the Irish nation,' de Valera led his followers from the chamber, leaving the pro-Treaty deputies to elect Griffith as the new President of the Dáil and of the Republic.

9
The Last Days

Griffith now faced a daunting task. Until the truce the Dáil had functioned as an underground organisation: the government had provided some alternative to the Castle administration and this had been surprisingly effective. Between truce and Treaty it had been concerned mainly with the question of negotiating a settlement. Now he had to build up a permanent system of government which would control virtually every aspect of life in Ireland, and he had to begin with a country ravaged by war, torn by dissension. There was reconstruction to be done, lost confidence in soldier-politicians to be regained, and democracy to be protected from those who were showing every sign of throttling it at birth.

The new cabinet was announced: Michael Collins (Finance), Gavan Duffy (Foreign Affairs), Eamonn Duggan (Home Affairs), Kevin O'Higgins (Economic Affairs), W. T. Cosgrave (Local Government) and Richard Mulcahy (Defence). When the opposition returned to the chamber, there was further wrangling. Who was to establish the Provisional Government? Griffith repeated his assurance that he would keep the Republic alive until the people decided, but it seemed to many that it would be anomalous for the republican Dáil to create the Provisional Government which would be pledged to destroy it.

Erskine Childers pressed Griffith on his 'curious and

ambiguous situation'. 'I will not reply to any damned Englishman in this Assembly,' snapped Griffith, no doubt releasing the pent-up dislike of Childers which had grown in London when Childers appeared to be monitoring the activities of the delegation and reporting privately to de Valera. Back in 1912, Griffith had written of Childers: 'The difference between Mr Childers and the majority of English liberals is that they think they can successfully trick Ireland into fighting England's battles and Mr Childers does not . . . he will understand us when we add that we know he has no love for Ireland. He desires the Irish question honestly settled in England's interest.'[1]

Later, Griffith's opinion altered and when Sean T. O'Kelly, the Dáil's representative in Paris between 1919 and 1921, asked for Childers to help win over some unfriendly French editors, Griffith sent him with a letter of warm praise.[2] O'Kelly was shocked by Griffith's outburst in the Dáil.

The 'curious and ambiguous situation' was resolved when Michael Collins was elected Chairman of the Provisional Government, in effect a working party, to which, under Article 17 of the Treaty, the British government was to transfer 'the powers and machinery requisite for the discharge of its duties'. For the election of the Provisional Government and formal ratification of the Treaty, the Dáil became, for one meeting, the parliament of Southern Ireland provided for under the Government of Ireland Act, 1920.

The new Provisional Government was, in theory at least, responsible to the Dáil, which remained the sovereign body. On 16 January, Collins led his team of ministers – Cosgrave, Duggan, O'Higgins, Mac Néill, Patrick Hogan, Fionan Lynch and Joseph McGrath – to Dublin Castle, supreme symbol of British domination of Ireland, to take over the administration. Several of his ministers held the same portfolio in Griffith's administration and were, rather incongruously, responsible to themselves.

Five days later, Collins reached an agreement with Sir James Craig. In return for Craig's promise to protect the Catholic minority in the six counties from persecution, Collins undertook to end the boycott on Belfast goods instituted in August 1920. Collins had also visited London several times to work out 'Heads of Working Arrangements for implementing the Treaty'. Churchill informed his colleagues that the Irish wanted a Free State government and an approved constitution in the shortest possible time.[3]

Tension could almost be felt when the Sinn Féin Ard Fheis was held on 21 February but there was no vote on the Treaty. Collins agreed to de Valera's suggestion that the election be delayed for three months. De Valera was convinced that, given a respite, the people would refuse to become a part of the British Empire or, more accurately, to continue a connection which until now they had been unable to break. Collins was confident of the support of the people but needed time to get the IRA on his side.

The IRA, bound by oath to the Republic and to the Dáil, were restive. Their responsibility now was to Mulcahy, who had assured the Dáil that the Army would remain the Army of the Irish Republic. The majority of the GHQ staff favoured the Treaty. Mulcahy was still Chief of Staff (but shortly afterwards handed over to Eoin O'Duffy) and Collins remained Director of Intelligence. They could count on O'Duffy, J. J. O'Connell, Gearoid O'Sullivan, Sean MacMahon, Emmet Dalton, Diarmuid O'Hegarty and Piaras Beaslai. Liam Mellows, Rory O'Connor, Sean Russell and Seamus O'Donovan were against the Treaty and they had the support of a number of divisional commandants, notably Liam Lynch.

The British withdrawal was quickening and the

British never knew whether they were handing over posts to IRA units which supported the Treaty or were extreme Republicans. Ernie O'Malley, commanding the Second Southern Division, repudiated the Treaty and GHQ, and raided Clonmel RIC barracks for arms. Churchill at once protested to Collins, who replied unkindly that the British 'ought to take more care in the distribution of lethal weapons to unauthorised persons.'[4] There was also trouble in Limerick and elsewhere and the possibility of civil war was frightening.

At first, the cabinet agreed that the Army might have a convention but, as trouble mounted, Griffith foresaw the possibility of a military coup d'etat and Mulcahy banned the meeting. He agreed with Griffith that the Army owed its loyalty to the Dáil, whatever the political views of individual members might be, but like Collins, he still hoped to prevent a breakaway. The prohibition offended more moderate Republicans who had hoped for a *modus vivendi* and threw them into the arms of the dissidents. The convention went ahead on 26 March, attended mostly by men who had decided against the Dáil. Those present reaffirmed their oath to the Republic, rejected the authority of the Minister for Defence and the Chief of Staff, and re-established the Army executive as the source of authority. The IRA was finally split.

Collins had worked frantically to maintain unity but in this he had little sympathy from Griffith. Griffith was also disappointed that Collins had agreed to postpone the election and was increasingly critical of Collins's various manoeuvres. Of the two men Griffith was much the more resolute at this time. For him, a lifetime's work, which had come very close to the goal he had set for himself in the early days of the century, now threatened to come to pieces in his hands. But Arthur Griffith, though he had worked with the IRA,

gone to prison with them, shared their triumphs and
[140] failures, had not been a comrade-in-arms. He was hurt when he was shunned by friends, but it was not the hurt of Collins whose friends had risked their lives with him and for him.

Both Griffith and Collins were deeply concerned about the North. There was trouble on the border and the Craig-Collins Pact had puttered out. IRA forces moved to the North to protect the minority of Catholic-nationalists and Collins saw to it that they were armed, taking steps to ensure that the weapons could not be identified as British. As sectarian violence flared, Collins doubted Craig's ability to control the situation. The measures Craig did take seemed to be aimed at the IRA rather than Protestant extremists and when Field Marshal Sir Henry Wilson, now a Unionist MP, and a known intriguer, was appointed as offical adviser to the controversial Special Constabulary, Collins's suspicions crystallised. Whilst refusing to give an inch on the working of the Treaty, he became deeply involved with its opponents in attempting to ameliorate the plight of his co-religionists. The part he played he kept from Griffith, but information reaching the British cabinet made them wary.

Collins was not trying to coerce the North, only to save Catholic lives, and he continued to seek a solution politically as well as militarily. IRA dissidents saw an opportunity to reunite the divided IRA by switching the emphasis from the Crown to partition, but in London, on 30 March, a second agreement was concluded between Craig and Lord Londonderry on the one hand and Griffith, Collins and Duggan on the other. The IRA's activities in the six counties were to cease and, in return, the Belfast police force was to be reorganised to include a proportion of Catholics in certain areas. But the religious feud continued and the lamentable Belfast Boycott was reimposed, not by the Dáil government but by the IRA, who were able to enforce it.

By 1 April, the transfer of powers to the Provisional Government had been completed and Ireland now had control of her finances, but, in the opinion of the British government, of not much else. Churchill told the cabinet that the Provisional Government would certainly try to work the Treaty but that they were faced with 'powerful and unscrupulous enemies'. He wrote to Collins to tell him that if he could not deal with the dissidents the British government would have to step in. At the same time, he explained to his own cabinet colleagues that Griffith and Collins believed the Treaty would be endangered if they struck the first blow against the Republicans. Churchill also warned them that 'any British military or police support at this stage would prove disastrous to the Provisional Government'.[5] In fact, nothing would have healed the rift in the IRA more quickly.

The British were afraid the Provisional Government might be overthrown and a republican government established. Advised by Macready, they were aware that the new National Army was not strong enough to prevent it. Arthur Griffith was also apprehensive and, under the strain, his health was deteriorating. He understood and respected the hostile views of those against the Treaty but, intent on establishing a democracy, he expected that opposition to be expressed in the Dáil. He was not prepared to tolerate a maverick army. De Valera had given him some comfort when he formed Cumann na Poblachta, or League of the Republic, which seemed to indicate that he at least intended the contest to stay in the political arena; but, at the same time, in various speeches in which he tried to warn the country of the horrors of civil war, de Valera seemed rather to be inciting it.

Making political speeches was a hazardous under-
[142] taking and both Griffith and Collins ran risks. Griffith spoke at Sligo on 16 April, Easter Sunday, despite a warning from the Mayor. The town was full of Republican troops, beginning to be called 'Irregulars' by the Treaty supporters and 'Executive Forces' by their own. Sean MacEoin brought a strong party of National troops from Athlone, outmanoeuvred the local Republican leader, escorted Griffith in an armoured car to the meeting and himself, with a gun in each hand, stood guard at a window over the street while Griffith addressed the crowd.

Two days earlier, Republicans led by Rory O'Connor seized the great building of the Four Courts and other Dublin buildings. O'Connor had made it clear that there would be no compromise. 'Some of us are no more prepared to stand for de Valera than for the Treaty,' he said. This was a deliberate challenge to the Provisional Government and there was now a real threat of government by a military junta, but Collins, to Griffith's perplexity and despair, persisted in his efforts to patch up the IRA split. He seemed to have succeeded when, on 1 May, after a number of amicable meetings, a group of ten prominent officers on both sides signed an agreement, the Army Document. The aim was to prevent a conflict which 'would be the greatest calamity in Irish history, and would leave Ireland broken for generations'. It recognised that the majority of the people were willing to accept the Treaty, provided for an agreed election leading to the formation of a government which would have the confidence of the whole country, and unification of the Army. A few days earlier, the Roman Catholic hierarchy had urged a meeting of leaders to hammer out a peaceful solution and the Army Document reflected the bishops' concern, though the inspiration came not from the church but from the officers themselves.

The men in the Four Courts would have none of the Army Document and there were clashes between the National Army and the Executive Forces in various parts of the country. The Dáil received a deputation of five signatories of the Army Document and listened to a moving plea from Sean O'Hegarty, who was not a Deputy. A Dáil Committee of ten, including Liam Mellows from the Four Courts and Tom Clarke's widow, who was a passionate opponent of the Treaty, came near enough to an agreement to enable Collins and de Valera to thrash out the final details. What emerged was the Collins-de Valera Pact, which envisaged a coalition government. When the election took place, there was to be a National Coalition Panel, each party being represented in proportion to its existing strength in the Dáil. The Executive would be made up of the President, the Minister of Defence representing the Army, plus five pro-Treaty and four anti-Treaty ministers. Candidates from other groups, such as Labour (which had not contested either the 1918 or 1921 elections so as not to weaken Sinn Féin, the freedom party) were free to stand against Panel candidates.

Griffith was incredulous and angry. 'You have given them everything,' he charged Collins, but, with Collins, Cosgrave and O'Higgins, he traipsed to London to explain the situation to the Colonial Secretary, Winston Churchill, who had written to Collins 'pointing out that such an election would be received with world wide ridicule and reprobation'. Churchill was critical of the failure to evict the Four Courts garrison, fearing that their intention might be to provoke the intervention of the British Army, and thus, inevitably, unite the broken IRA. The Irish delegation put their case well, and although Churchill still held that the Pact was a threat to democracy, he explained to his colleagues that 'the idea was to try and get a non-party

government so as to secure tranquillity in Ireland and
[144] at a later date a proper election on the main issue.'[6]

If the Pact was to have any chance of working, the new constitution had to be drafted so that it absolved de Valera and his supporters from pledging fealty to the King and from any acknowledgment of the Treaty, for otherwise they would not take their seats in the Dáil. De Valera envisaged the continuation of the Dáil, which still represented the Republic, and the gradual attrition of the Provisional Government. Chaired by Darrell Figgis, a committee had been working on the Constitution for some time. It was not a happy committee. Figgis clashed with one member, Professor Alfred O'Rahilly, whose appointment, Figgis told Griffith in a letter, dated 24 February, had brought 'nothing but disorder'.[7] Only 'the strongest sense of duty' restrained him from resigning. Figgis suggested that Griffith might discuss with another member of the committee, Hugh Kennedy KC, with whom he would be travelling overnight (presumably to London), certain 'delicate situations' which had arisen and which 'you may be able to deal with in your own tactful way'.

The committee's work on the constitution disappointed the British cabinet.[8] The constitution was, in Churchill's words, a 'negation of the Treaty'. He was determined that the Irish should stick to their bargain, but was keenly aware that the lives of Collins and Griffith were at risk and was 'anxious not to put upon them more than they could bear'. Indeed, the strain was telling on both; Collins was often morose, Griffith short-tempered. Lloyd George told his cabinet colleagues that Griffith had suggested that he, Lloyd George, and de Valera, 'should share the government of Ireland between them, as if one was as impossible as the other'. For Griffith there had been no let-up for eight months. There had been the long, arduous

Treaty negotiations with the wily and experienced British, the disappointment of de Valera's repudiation of his efforts, and his own defence of them in the character-scarring debate in the Dáil. Endlessly he had journeyed to London for discussions with the British, while the IRA broke up and violence flared in Ulster as well as in the South. In the country, he had defended the Treaty from dangerous rostrums. He had to cope with a curious dichotomous form of government; President of the Republic, he was committed to masterminding the building of a permanent state in which the Republic would be disestablished. Inexorably, the country was moving towards civil war, but he could not persuade Michael Collins to take a firm stand against his intractable comrades. The men in the Four Courts, in defiance of any government, went their own way. Deeply anxious about the Catholic-nationalist minority in the North, Griffith could not condone Collins's involvement. The Collins-de Valera Pact had been sprung on him and now there was the row with the British over the constitution. He scarcely saw his wife and children. When he did, he was too tired and too preoccupied to enjoy them. The friendships which had meant so much to him were broken or neglected. His health was declining and he had no peace of mind. Little wonder that he promised his wife to retire from politics in August.

However, he was not beaten yet and set himself to reply to the memorandum containing the British objections to the constitution. In a way, Birkenhead had prepared the ground for him, explaining to the cabinet the complexity of drafting a treaty which would accurately interpret the Treaty. In a careful, lucid reply, every line of which manifested the integrity of its author, Griffith explained that the draft constitution was 'the work of an independent Com-

mittee acting upon their own independent interpretation
[146] tion of the Treaty and approaching it with minds biassed in its favour'.[9] To the six points raised in the British memorandum he gave reasoned answers and concluded that, where it could be shown that the draft constitution was at variance with the Treaty, amendments would be made. The British were satisfied and in one or two instances modified their demands, largely at Birkenhead's behest, though, rather surprisingly, Lloyd George supported him. 'It has to be remembered,' he said, 'that the Crown has too often in Ireland represented repression.' Nevertheless, in recent cabinet discussions, he had made it clear that if the issue should once again become that of Republic versus Empire, the matter would have to be settled by force of arms. For that reason, he was anxious that the troubles in the North should be settled and eliminated from the equation, for if the British public saw that as the main bone of contention, their support for armed action against the South could not be counted on.

Griffith and Collins had interlarded the constitution discussions with frequent worried references to the uproar in Belfast, which they saw as a bar to stability in the South. They urged an impartial inquiry into the violence, holding that Craig's 48,000 'Specials' were fomenting trouble. In their turn, the British were suspicious of IRA activity and, not without reason, of Collins himself. Griffith insisted that the responsiblity for order in the six counties was Britain's. Lloyd George, genuinely apprehensive of world opinion, was anxious to show that Britain was dealing impartially with the situation, and promised action.

Griffith was relieved on that score and was ready to face the electorate. Collins was still mistrustful. Both knew that the constitution they had finally accepted spelled the end of the Collins-de Valera Pact.

They had gone to London with a constitution which squared with de Valera's external association concept; they were returning with a draft, still to be settled in detail, which confirmed all that he objected to in the Treaty. In Cork, on 14 June, two days before the election, Collins urged the electors 'to vote for the candidates you think best of. . . .' He did not renounce the Pact but tacitly was acknowledging that it was dead.

His reason was obvious enough when the constitution was published on the morning of the election. The details had been finally settled only the previous day. That it had been deliberately withheld was a natural claim for the Republicans to make. In fact, the aim of the Provisional Government had been to give the British as short a time as possible to argue about the constitution, but the British had called their bluff.

Publication of the constitution earlier could have made very little difference since it reflected the terms of the Treaty and the real issue was whether or not the people accepted the Treaty. Overwhelmingly they did, for the anti-Treaty panel candidates polled only 133,864 of the 620,283 votes cast. The pro-Treaty panel candidates received 239,193 votes. Most significant of all were the 247,226 votes won by Labour, Independents and Farmers. In giving their verdict for the Treaty the people had added a rider. They were tired of warring factions and disenchanted with the dominance of military men in the Dáil. They wanted an end to the old arguments and, with their new found freedom, a chance to rebuild their country in peace.

In the new Dáil, Arthur Griffith's pro-Treaty Sinn Féin party would have fifty-eight seats against the thirty-five of the anti-Treaty party. Labour had won seventeen and were to bring a refreshing touch to the Dáil when eventually it met. Independents and

Farmers each had won seven seats and there were
[148] also four Unionists elected by Dublin University (Trinity College).

Arthur Griffith was never to take his seat. He knew that civil war was imminent. 'Pierce, we will have to fight,' he told Piaras Beaslai. Events crowded one upon another in the next weeks. On 22 June, less than a week after the election, Field Marshal Sir Henry Wilson was assassinated. Collins was convinced that Wilson was at the root of the pogrom (the word was used by Lloyd George himself) against Catholics in the North, and may have ordered Wilson's death in the belief that he was saving Catholic lives. Ernest Blythe, who was present when Collins helped an appalled Griffith prepare a statement deploring the killing, says that Collins was as disturbed as Griffith, although Blythe formed the impression that 'he had more information about it than his senior colleague.'[10]

At an emergency conference of ministers in London, Churchill drafted, and Lloyd George signed, a strong protest to Collins as Chairman of the Provisional Government. The British blamed 'the irregular elements of the IRA' for the attack and, in the House of Commons on 26 June, Churchill warned that, 'if through weakness, want of courage or some other less creditable reason' the occupation of the Four Courts was not brought to an end, the British government would regard the Treaty as 'having been formally violated.'

Collins's reaction was to snap that Churchill could do his own dirty work, but Collins's hand was forced when, also on 26 June, the Four Courts men kidnapped the National Army's Deputy Chief of Staff, General J. J. 'Ginger' O'Connell, in retaliation for the arrest of one of their men who was leading a raid to commandeer transport for operations in the North. Now that the Provisional Government had the people's sanction, they could not afford not to govern. They had to restore order, and it was imperative that the Four Courts enclave be eliminated. Griffith had recognised this from the beginning, and the kidnapping of O'Connell, cocking a snook at the National Army as it did, at last convinced GHQ that there could be no accommodation with the Executive Forces.

At a meeting of the Provisional Government and National Army leaders on 27 June, it was decided that 'notices should be served on the armed men in illegal occupation of the Four Courts and Fowler Hall that night, ordering them to evacuate the buildings and to surrender up all arms and property, and that in the event of their refusing to do so, the necessary military action would be taken at once.'[11]

The ultimatum was rejected and, in the early hours of 28 June, with four eighteen-pounder guns borrowed from the British, the National Army began its assault. It was hoped the artillery would demoralise the garrison and that damage to the building would be slight. Arthur Griffith watched the bombardment from a rooftop and his feelings must have been very mixed. Not until the afternoon of 30 June, after they had been driven into one section of the building, did the garrison surrender. Earlier, fire had reached their store of explosives and the Public Record Office, which was housed in the Four Courts, blew up with the loss of priceless records dating back to the twelfth century. There was more fighting in O'Connell Street (then Sackville Street) where Executive Forces had occupied a number of hotels, and in other parts of the city, and Dublin was not quiet until 6 July. O'Connell Street was by then a shambles; over sixty lives had been lost, including that of Cathal Brugha, who died with fanatical courage rather than surrender.

The Four Courts battle had precipitated action in many parts of the country. It was clear now that the

split in the IRA was irremediable. The National Army
[150] called for recruits. On 13 July a War Council of three, decided upon the previous evening, was announced. Urged by Mulcahy, Collins decided to 'go into uniform', becoming Commander-in-Chief of the Army. In his absence on military duties, Cosgrave was to act as Chairman of the Provisional Government. Mulcahy and O'Duffy, with Collins, made up the War Council.

Griffith, with other members of the government, was living in Government Buildings. He seemed at last to be almost spent. His face was ashen and the lines seemed to deepen with every sleepless night. His younger colleagues drew from the deep wells of his wisdom and experience, but missed his geniality. If Griffith was aware of the shadow creeping over his life, he must often have allowed his mind to wander back over the years he had given to Ireland's cause. That his efforts had ended in civil war must have been heart-breaking. He was spared the worst of it, the nine awful months of burning and killing, when some of Ireland's finest young men, including Michael Collins himself, died tragically and needlessly, leaving a legacy of such bitterness that traces linger yet. But neither was he privileged to live to see all, or nearly all, that he had striven for gradually achieved, by men that he had known in the clandestine government of the war years and by the next generation.

Oliver St John Gogarty, his friend and physician, recommended rest and Griffith went for a few days to St Vincent's hospital, though he still went to his office each day. On 12 August 1922, in the hospital corridor, he bent to tie a shoelace, collapsed and died at once of a cerebral haemorrhage.

Michael Collins hastened back to Dublin from a tour of National Army units in the south. Indirectly, Griffith's death brought about his own, for had his tour not been interrupted, the freakish near-accident that caused his death in the valley of Béal na mBláth, only ten days later, would never have occurred.

In his uniform of Commander-in-Chief, Collins led Griffith's sad procession through crowded, silent streets to Glasnevin. Arthur Griffith was buried as Head of State, but the new Dáil had not been able to meet, the constitution had not been passed, the Free State was not yet in being. He was still President of the Republic of Ireland. The anomaly worried the British cabinet, to whom he was 'merely President of the Dáil, though connected with a Government which was fighting a loyal battle so far as the Crown was concerned.' They were reminded of his 'firm and loyal attitude towards the treaty'. The King was advised to send a personal note of condolence to Mrs Griffith; an official note, signed by the Prime Minister and the other Treaty signatories on the British side, was sent to Michael Collins.

The Irish were less concerned with the niceties. There was grief but men said what they thought.

In a letter to his benefactor, E. R. (later Sir Ernest) Debenham, Stephen Mackenna wrote: 'Poor Art O'Griovha, a lifelong friend, had to my mind made such a chaos of Ireland as must cloud his eternity.'

In the Senate, some months after Griffith's death, W. B. Yeats paid his tribute: 'I was on many points deeply opposed to Mr Arthur Griffith during his life-time on matters connected with the arts, but time has justified him on the great issue that most concerns us all. . . .'

References

Chapter 1: The Matrix (pp. 1-9)

1. Warner and Marten, *The Groundwork of British History* (III), 579.
2. ibid.
3. Padraic Colum, *Arthur Griffith,* 19.
4. National Library of Ireland (NLI), MS 3493.
5. Robert Kee, *The Green Flag,* 384.
6. Seán Ó Lúing, *Art Ó Gríofa,* 25.
7. Colum, 21. 8. ibid., 28.

Chapter 2: Home Thoughts from Abroad (pp. 10-31)

1. Colum, 34. 2. ibid., 35.
3. George A. Lyons, *Recollections of Arthur Griffith,* 13.
4. ibid., 18. 5. ibid., 19. 6. ibid., 21.
7. *United Irishman,* 10/10/'03
8. Colum, 47. 9. ibid., 57. 10. ibid., 66.
11. *United Irishman,* 1/11/'02
12. Michael Collins, *The Path to Freedom,* 125.
13. P. S. O'Hegarty, *Sunday Independent,* 12/8/'45
14. General R. Mulcahy, private note.
15. Sean T. O'Kelly, *The Capuchin Annual,* 1966
16. ibid.
17. H. A. L. Fisher, *A History of Europe,* 1036.
18. Ó Lúing, 407. 19. Kee, 33.
20. Bulmer Hobson, *Ireland Yesterday and Tomorrow,* 8
21. Ó Lúing, 131. 22. Colum, 32. 23. Ó Lúing, 142.
24. Hobson, 12. 25. General Mulcahy, private memo.
26. Hobson, 23. 27. ibid., 10.
28. P. S. O'Hegarty, *A History of Ireland Under the Union,* 643.
29. NLI, MS 21750. 30. *Sinn Féin,* 3/6/'11.
31. *United Irishman,* 10/10/'03. 32. ibid., 24/10/'03.

Chapter 3: Irish Stew (pp. 32-52)

1. Colum, 93. 2. ibid., 97. 3. ibid., 98.
4. NLI, MS 18255. 5. Richard Davis, *Arthur Griffith and Non-Violent Sinn Féin*, 60.
6. James Stephens, *Arthur Griffith, Journalist and Statesman, 18.*
7. NLI, MS 10872.
8. Seamus O'Sullivan, *Essays and Recollections*, 104.
9. Seamus O'Sullivan, *The Rose and Bottle*, 9.
10. Ó Lúing, 18. 11. Davis, 62. 12. Ó Lúing, 201.
13. NLI, MS 5943. 14. General Mulcahy, private note.
15. Patrick Buckland, *James Craig*, 24. 16. Colum, 110.
17. *Sinn Féin*, 18/8/'14. 18. Colum, 131.
19. Francis Shaw, *Studies*, Summer 1972.

Chapter 4: The Easter Rising (pp. 53-59)

1. O'Kelly, *Capuchin*, 1966. 2. General Mulcahy, private note.
3. NLI, MS 18975.
4. Public Record Office, London, PM's report to King, cabinet meeting, 6/5/'16.

Chapter 5: The New Sinn Féin (pp. 60-75)

1. O'Kelly, *Capuchin*. 2. NLI, MS 18975.
3. Arthur Griffith to Lil Williams, 5/8/'16, NLI, MS 5943.
4. Colum, 159. 5. AG to LW 5/8/'16.
6. Arthur Griffith to Flo Williams (undated), MS 5943
7. AG to LW 29/11/'16, MS 5943
8. PRO, PM to King, cabinet meeting, 19/7/'16.
9. AG to FW, MS 5943. 10. O'Kelly, *Capuchin*, 1966.
11. PRO, war cabinet minute 311(5), 13/2/'18.
12. WC mins 353(3), 25/2/'18 and 354(8), 26/2/'18.
13. WC min. 375(2), 27/3/'18. 14. Colum, 181.
15. PRO, cabinet paper GT 4218.
16. William O'Brien, *The Irish Revolution*, 361-2
17. WC min. 395(13), 19/4/'18. 18. NLI, MS 5943.
19. Colum, 189. 20. NLI, MS 15790.
21. NLI, MS 10872. 22. Colum, 191.

Chapter 6: Fight for Freedom (pp. 76-100)

1. Colum, 190.
2. Longford and O'Neill, *Eamon de Valera*, 95.
3. Colum, 204.
4. PRO, cabinet conclusion, 79A, 27/12/'20.

5. Colum, 239. 6. ibid., 224.
7. Cabinet paper, CP 2829, 13/4/'21.
8. Cabinet conclusion, 60/21(1), 20/7/'21. 9. ibid.
10. Sir Nevil Macready, *Annals of an Active Life*, 585.
11. Cabinet paper CP 3204, 7-8/8/'21.
12. Longford and O'Neill, 145.
13. ibid., 147.

Chapter 7: The Talk of London (pp. 101-120)

1. Kathleen Napoli McKenna, *The Capuchin Annual*, 1971.
2. PRO, cabinet conclusion 74/21(1), 7/9/'21.
3. Colum, 285. 4. Frank Pakenham, *Peace by Ordeal*, 217
5. Colum, 296. 6. ibid.
7. J. L. Hammond, *C. P. Scott of the Manchester Guardian*, 284.
8. McKenna, *Capuchin*.
9. Cabinet conclusion 23/22, 5/4/'22.
10. Colum, 304. 11. ibid., 305.

Note: Documents in PRO, London, CAB 43, Conferences on Ireland: record of Treaty negotiations (22N143) and documents (SF series) also extensively used without specific references being made.

Chapter 8: Ideals in Conflict (pp. 121-135)

1. Longford and O'Neill, 167. 2. Colum, 306.
3. Leon Ó Broin, *Michael Collins*, 113. 4. Colum, 307.
5. T. Ryle Dwyer, *Eamon de Valera*, quoting Dáil Éireann private debate, 44.
6. PRO, cabinet conclusion, 91/21(1), 7/12/'21.
7. General Mulcahy, note of conversation with Dr Conor Cruise O'Brien, 28/12/'62.
8. Dwyer, 44. 9. Professor Michael Hayes in interview.

Chapter 9: The Last Days (pp. 136-151)

1. *Sinn Féin*, 9/8/'12. 2. O'Kelly, *Capuchin*.
3. PRO, cabinet conclusion, 3/22(4), 23/1/'22.
4. ibid., 16/22(1), 8/3/'22.
5. Cabinet conclusion, 23/22, 5/4/'22.
6. Cabinet conclusion, 30/22(3), 30/5/'22.
7. NLI, MS 18551.
8. Cabinet conclusion, 30/22(3), 30/5/'22.
9. Cabinet paper, CP 4014 II, 2/6/'22.
10. Ernest Blythe, *Irish Times*, 19/11/'68.
11. General Mulcahy, record of meeting, 27/6/'22.

Index